Life and Soul

Life and Soul:
New Light on a Sublime Mystery

by
Thomas G. Casey, S.J.

Templegate Publishers
Springfield, Illinois

First published in 2005 by
Templegate Publishers, LLC
302 East Adams Street
P.O. Box 5152
Springfield, Illinois 62705-5152
217-522-3353
templegate.com

© 2005 Thomas G. Casey

ISBN 0-87243-267-X
Library of Congress Control Number 2005929737

De licentia superiorum ordinis

Cover: William Blake's *The Angel Invites Dante to Enter the Flames*
from *The Divine Comedy*

For my newly-born niece Rachel:
may you have the beauty of soul that never ages.

Contents

Acknowledgements

"To hell or to Connacht!"
                                            Oliver Cromwell (1599-1658)

Oliver Cromwell, the famous seventeenth-century English military and political leader, thought little of the Irish province of Connacht. To those Irish landowners who opposed him, he presented the stark choice between a one-way ticket to hell or permanent banishment to the barren land west of the River Shannon, which included the province of Connacht as well as County Clare in Munster. Recently I had the opportunity to visit the county of Clare in a voluntary capacity. Travelling along its winding roads and patchwork fields with hundreds of shades of green, where cows graze nonchalantly next to ruins from the Stone Age, I found my sentiments differing radically from those of Cromwell. The experience of this quintessentially Irish landscape gave a heavenly direction to my thoughts. But not so much because of the ancient landscape I saw; more on account of the mystical country I did not see.

I was visiting with some friends in Kilkee, County Clare, a holiday town cosily tucked into a sheltered bay on the west coast. I had heard that the cliffs and coastline of this corner of the country were majestic and magical; but a

9

thick blanket of fog had descended over both land and water that very afternoon, and seemed destined to remain there immovably and forever. We could barely see more than fifty yards in front of us. The air carried the purifying taste of salt water to our lips from the vast expanse of the Atlantic Ocean that we knew stretched out before us. But the fog had successfully concealed it from our sight. Indeed even the horse-shoe shaped bay immediately in front of us yielded little to our searching eyes. We could only discern the ghostliness of shifting shapes as we gazed around us in the gathering twilight. Not that we had the leisure to stand there for long. The gentle drizzle intermittently whipped up into a wind-driven frenzy, and then the raindrops would stab us like so many pine needles while the wind itself would hit us with the sudden force of some invisible and mythical Irish monster.

The glimpses that I got through that mist-covered landscape reminded me of the inklings of eternity that my soul has been privileged to receive. At many special moments in my life I have been lucky to catch sight of my true destination through the confusing fog of the everyday. Because of God's illumination that has come to me through the affection of friends and mentors, through the regular rhythm of prayer and reflection, and through the nourishment of sacrament and scripture, I have realized that God has a marvellous destiny awaiting each one of us, even if we now only have occasionally unclouded instances of clarity when we can see where happiness and harmony await us. But if we can wake up to these moments, they will be enough to encourage us to yearn deeply for what "no eye has seen, no ear has heard, no mind has conceived what God has prepared for those who love him" (1 Corinthians 2:9). In gratitude for this rich tapestry of grace that has threaded its way through my life in myriad ways, I decided to write this book on the soul.

I would like to thank Mary, Joe, Cynthia, John, Cecilia, Iggy and Az for the wonderful gift of their friendship, a testimony to the power of our spiritual nature, replete as it is with luminous presence and deep fruitfulness. Finally, and most of all, I would like to thank God for the gift of the soul, this pearl without price.

Introduction

"Through a chink too wide there comes in no wonder."

Patrick Kavanagh, "Advent"

The soul is "in" again. In one of those frequent ironies of history, the less Christians talk about the soul, the more other religious seekers turn to this word to express something of their sense of the indefinable and sacred mystery of the person. Of course the soul was never really out of fashion in the first place: from the dawn of human history, women and men have asked themselves who they are and what their place is in the world; and in the process they have also wondered about the soul. As he lay on his deathbed overlooking the beautiful Bay of Naples in 138 A.D., the Roman Emperor Hadrian composed a farewell poem to his soul. Hadrian was the most powerful man in the world at that time, with an empire that extended from the wall named after him in Scotland to the land of Iran. But however great the achievements that were to outlive him—Rome still boasts his Castel Sant' Angelo on the River Tiber—he now realized that he too was mortal. Once it was separated from his body, he was convinced his soul would become small and defenceless, losing the strength necessary for happiness and vitality. Hadrian the great statesman voices his vulnerability in this little poem:

> Little gentle bewildered soul
> Guest and companion of the body
> Who now prepares you to descend to places
>   that are colourless, cold and bare
> Never more will you abandon yourself to your
>   favourite games.[1]

The musings of humanity about the soul reverberate in ancient songs and stories, they thread their way through legends and myths, they are hammered into sculptures and mingle mysteriously with the fine brushwork of the greatest paintings. The great Michelangelo Buonarotti (1475-1564), for example, was fascinated by the human figure not so much on account of its anatomy but because of the soul that surged from its depths. Michelangelo's *Pietà*, the only sculpture he ever signed, shows the poignant grief of a mother's soul. His monumental statue *David*, the original of which stood for centuries in the main square of Florence, manifests the inner strength of soul that is more powerful than the might of Goliath. His rough-hewn blocks of marble stone in the Accademia in Florence, containing slaves struggling to break free of the material that surrounds them, evoke souls yearning for the infinite and trying to liberate themselves from the multiple forms of slavery that tie down human beings. The four allegorical statues that Michelangelo sculpted for the tombs of the Medici family in Florence—the reclining figures of *Twilight, Dawn, Night* and *Day*—capture something of the suffering of the soul in the face of the vicissitudes of life. And all great sculpture, painting, music and literature are attempts to wrest meaning from the flux of history, to create something permanent and lasting from what is fleeting and transient—thereby they are witnesses to the soul, this immortal treasure which transcends the limits of space and time.

But in modern times many intellectuals have radically questioned the very notion of the soul. Indeed the pervasive tendency to explain human behaviour in terms of evolutionary theory and scientific models of reality has led ordinary people to wonder whether the soul exists any more. Many Christian theologians have become embarrassed by the soul, as though it were an outdated relic from a bygone age, and have become correspondingly bashful about discussing it. Yet for all that, humanity's fascination with the soul has not diminished: walk into any bookshop and you will see countless self-help and therapeutic books that use the word "soul" in their titles. Jack Canfield and Mark Victor Hansen have penned a series of bestsellers that offer "chicken soup for the soul". James Hillman and Thomas Moore return to the theme of the soul again and again.[2] John O'Donohue's exquisitely written book on Celtic spirituality, *Anam Cara*, uses the Gaelic word for "soul" [*anam*] in its title.[3] Despite the fact that few Christian theologians feel the urgency of writing about the soul, there is a huge number of New Age and inspirational writers who cannot talk enough about it. Deepak Chopra notes that:

> . . . the fact of the soul appears to be undeniable, for stripped of all religious connotations, the essence of each person cannot be reduced to matter or thoughts or any fixed quality.[4]

But the undeniable and overwhelming interest that contemporary writers show for the soul has not succeeded in
giving it clarity, much less unveiling its essential mystery;
the soul remains stubbornly opaque and tantalizingly elusive. We are left with more questions than answers.

Do human beings consist of matter alone? Or is there
something immaterial in the human being that loves and
chooses, that thinks and understands? Are body and soul
simply added together in an external way like butter and
jam in a sandwich? Or is the soul intimately connected with
the body? Does the soul outlive the body? The number of
questions that can be asked about the soul is vast. But the
answers that can be provided are smaller in number and
necessarily humble. Christian theology contends that the
soul exists, just as scientists affirm that the universe exists.
But as for the nature of the soul, theologians can only offer
modest suggestions, just as scientists offer tentative
hypotheses about the nature of the universe. The soul is a
universe in itself and a mystery. It is invisible. That is why
the best way to see the soul is through its effects upon our
lives.

The reason I believe the soul is worth studying is that the
soul makes the human being an absolutely unique creature in
our world. Human beings enjoy a qualitatively higher level
of being than any other living thing on earth. The human
soul designates this height, nobility and particularity of
humans, who are the only creatures to be created in God's
likeness. This is not to say that only human beings have
souls. The Book of Genesis tells us that each animal has a
living soul (Genesis 1:30). In order to better highlight the
unique nature of the human soul, I want to contrast it briefly
with the animal soul. Although I stress the differences

between human beings and the rest of the animal world, there are thinkers who prefer to stress their similarities.[5] The ongoing debate about the degree of resemblance between humans and other animals is outside the scope of my study—I will not compare and contrast the human soul and the animal soul with a view to fuelling this debate. The reason I specifically contrast human life with other animal life is to throw into sharper relief what it is that sets human beings apart. At the same time let me clarify where I stand on the debate about the similarities between humans and other animals. On the one hand, I see continuity between animals and human beings: both animals and human beings *are*. But this continuity does not imply sameness. Human beings are further along the spectrum of being which they share with animals, precisely because of *what* humans are. Despite undeniable similarities between humans and animals, humans have a more complex nature than animals do. This more complex nature is reflected in human behaviour and actions, which are more sophisticated and complex than the activities of their animal counterparts, despite certain undeniable similarities.

This sophistication and complexity show the nobility of the human soul. Of course the human soul itself cannot be seen; it remains invisible. But it can be discerned in everything that differentiates us from animals. For instance, although all animals communicate, and some even transmit messages in sophisticated ways, only human beings use language to convey their thoughts. Anyone who has taught a pet parrot an amusing phrase knows that although this bird has an uncanny ability to imitate human pronunciation, it does not know what it is saying. But when we articulate our thoughts, our soul reveals itself. The sounds that animals use to communicate have nothing of the rich variation of human language: for instance, the barking of an Alsatian in Pakistan is no different from the barking of an Alsatian in Peru. But the language of the Pakistani people differs greatly from the language of Peruvians. Despite its distinctive beauty, the sad sweet song of the nightingale is always the same; but not every human being sings like Luciano Pavarotti. Animals learn how to communicate by nature; although communication is natural to human beings as well, they also acquire all sorts of signs and sounds from their particular cultures, which is why for instance Neapolitans have the uncanny ability to talk with their hands.

The human soul is so intimately linked with the human body that when the person dies and the body decomposes, the soul survives only in an incomplete manner through God's benevolence, until it is reunited with its glorified body. The link between the animal soul and animal body is much closer, so much so that it would seem the animal's soul cannot exist without its physical body. In other words, the soul of the animal apparently dies with its body.[6]

Animals may be mortal, but they are far from dumb and are certainly not as ignorant as some people presume. They have a kind of knowledge that is focused on the particular things they perceive with their senses. By means of sensation the animal picks up information and knowledge about specific things in the world. With its external senses, the animal, like the human being, can see and hear, smell, taste and touch. The internal senses of the animal include memory, imagination, instinct and meaning-giving functions. The horse remembers its master; the dog barks at night in response to imagined danger; baby ducklings instinctively follow their mother; the panther puts together the sensory information it receives and perceives a white-tailed deer in front of it.

Like the panther, the human being combines sensory data to perceive a particular deer but human knowledge also runs deeper. The powerfully-built panther springs upon its prey; the human being makes a longer journey of exploration. I can endeavour to understand the deer I see fifty yards away in the forest by asking what it is and what makes it the particular animal that it is. The knowledge I gain also enriches and augments me. Through the mystery of human knowledge I can receive this panther into myself. Of course the panther still retains its independent existence outside of me, so that I do not swallow it up. Yet it also miraculously exists inside of me, receiving a new existence as it were. In the process I become more than myself. The horizons of my world are enlarged. How can I encompass so much or stretch myself to such immense dimensions? The answer is given by my soul: the fact that so many realities outside of me can also find a dwelling within me and that I can "become" what is other points to the limitless vastness of the soul.

Unlike the panther, I can abstract from the particular deer in front of me and I can form the concept "deer" which I can then apply to any number of ruminant mammals with two large and two small hooves on each foot, most of the males of which have solid branched antlers which are shed annually. As distinct from the panther whose knowledge is purely geared toward consumption since it will devour the deer as soon as it can, my intellect can reverence this beautiful animal. This respectful stance is evidenced by naturalists and zoologists who devote so much time to studying deer, to protecting them and their natural habitats. They try to divine the essence of the deer so that they can better allow these mammals to thrive and flourish. They seek to know and understand deer without the ulterior motive of appropriating them for egoistic ends.

As for human memory, it goes beyond the remembrance of specific things and helps the person remember that they are a self, someone with a distinct and unique identity. As I remember my past actions I also recall that it was *I* who carried them out. And so with the help of memory I gather myself into a meaningful whole with a continuous existence. Because of memory I do not lose the past and therefore I do not lose myself for thanks to memory I can paradoxically still be what I no longer am. An excellent example of the particular memory opening onto something more primordial is to be found in a key episode from the first volume of Marcel Proust's (1871-1922) massive novel *Remembrance of Things Past*. One afternoon, against habit, the narrator drinks a cup of tea with a piece of madeleine cake, a small sweet pastry. As soon as he recognizes its taste and aroma, he recalls that as a child his aunt Léonie used to dip a piece of madeleine into her cup of tea on Sunday mornings at Combray before giving it to her young nephew. Immediately his memories of childhood come flooding back and the reader in turn becomes immersed in a novel of memory that produces a sublime vision which defies the vagaries of time.

The imagination of the animal has nothing of the richness and variety of human imagination. In the twinkling of an eye I can picture the Eiffel Tower, fly around it, turn it upside down, colour it green, and cover it with confetti. More significantly, with the help of the imagination I can envisage a new and better world, actively resisting the paralysis of fate to embrace the dynamism of a liberating future. Michelangelo saw perfect forms in even the most recalcitrant blocks of stone and marble and with his hands and chisel set about the process of liberating them. The foundational story of Jesus' death and resurrection, which is at the heart of Christianity, stimulates the ethical imagination. This dynamic truth helps Christians to understand the world and themselves in a better way, giving them power to make both themselves and the world new.

A moving example of the power of human memory and imagination is contained in Jean-Dominique Bauby's *The Diving Bell and the Butterfly: A Memoir of Life in Death.*[7] The author, an erstwhile editor of the French *Elle* magazine, suffered a stroke that left his mind functioning but his body completely paralyzed except for movement in one eyelid. He dictated this book by blinking out the letters of each word with his left eye. The title of his memoir refers both to his immobility and freedom: because of his paralysis he felt as though he were trapped inside a diving bell while simultaneously his mind stayed as free as a butterfly and as capricious in its flights of fancy. Despite the horror of his illness, Bauby's book is a testament to the power of the human soul to soar above bodily adversity and to affirm life with the help of memory and imagination. Were an animal in a similarly horrendous situation, it would simply shrivel up and die.

It is because of the soul that human beings have the audacity and capacity to love forever. The animal has an instinctive love which is why a mother swan will risk her own life defending her cygnets. The animal also has a sensible love that directs it towards things that it perceives to be good: the lion associates the taste of buffalo with pleasure.

An animal can display lifelong loyalty and devotion by allowing itself to be tamed and ruled over by its owner in order to serve the human being, thereby fulfilling the purpose for which it was created.[8] Only a human being can love in a conscious and intentional way rather than in a merely instinctive or sensible manner, and this love again shows the soul. The human being has a sensible love which may lead to great pleasure in rich food; but the human can also temper these pleasures and abstain from eating for higher motives. The human being can certainly respond instinctively in self-defence but can also go beyond instinct by deciding to turn the other cheek or more, like the Franciscan priest St. Maximilian Kolbe who offered his life for another prisoner in Auschwitz in 1941.

The soul is the vital principle in the human being, by which the person lives and realizes the various activities of life, especially the conscious activities of thinking and willing. The soul is the principle of life in the animal too, though this life does not have the same breadth or depth as human life. The animal has the ability to grow and develop, ingesting and absorbing food, the power to reproduce, and the capacity to respond to external stimuli. The life of the animal follows a repetitive and monotonous pattern of eating, sleeping, hunting, and reproducing itself. Human life is characterized by a vast variety of activities: we can choose to eat all sorts of exotic foods, we can ration sleep, we can engage in a wide spectrum of pastimes, and so on. But animal life, bereft as it is of self-consciousness, cannot escape monotony: the cow never rises above the green-meadow gregariousness of bovine mediocrity. The life of the animal never attains the spiritual, intellectual, affective or social heights of human life.

It is by virtue of the soul that we can live for God and become like him. Although an animal can be physically beautiful, only a human being can grow beautiful in goodness, and this goodness manifests the soul, this unfathomable mystery that pervades our being. An animal can display something analogous to this inner beauty by actively followed the instinct implanted in it by God. But the perfection of nature to which the soul invites each person is beyond the ken of any animal and surpasses even our own deepest imaginings. We humans are soul creatures, because at the core of our being we are grounded in God, however much we try to tear up these divine roots. Of course, we can never extricate these roots altogether from within ourselves, precisely because they sink into a foundation without foundation, into the very abyss of God.

There is an intricate and involved relationship between the soul and the body. The human being is neither merely body nor only soul. On the other hand, the human being is not simply the addition of body and soul. Nor should we say that the human being has a body and has a soul. Rather, the human being is entirely body and entirely soul, a body that is penetrated to the core by spirit, a soul that is embodied. Yet for all that, body and soul are not identical. We can make certain distinctions between the two, as long as we remember that the precision and neat separation these distinctions promise cannot be recaptured at the level of lived life.

As entirely body, the human being is mortal; as entirely soul, immortal. As entirely body, the human being is of this world; as entirely soul, the human being transcends this world. As entirely body, the human being is visible; as entirely soul, the human being is invisible. As entirely body,[9] the human being is determined; as entirely soul, the human being is free. But such contrasts do not imply that body and soul are two contrasting entities that exist side by side in an indifferent or accidental manner. However, such contrasts do imply that body and soul fall short of being in utter communion. They are intertwined and reciprocally influence one another, though without being one another. However, in our everyday lives, before the process of explicit reflection, we generally experience them as a unity.

This pre-reflective unity of body and soul is analogous to the wisdom expressed in the question that concludes William Butler Yeats' poem "Among School Children": "how can we know the dancer from the dance?" In this poem, the aging Yeats, now recognized throughout Ireland as a leading poet, visits an elementary school in Dublin, and while walking through the long classroom with a smile, finds that behind his benign public face, he is agonizing over some of life's most fundamental questions. The question that ends Yeats' poem is not so much a rational question that will lead to a clear answer as an imaginative question that stimulates thought. By asking whether we can "know the dancer from the dance," he seems to be suggesting that separating one from the other is impossible. In other words, there is such a deep unity between art and the artist that he or she becomes totally engrossed in the act of creating and so practically inseparable from it. In a similar sense, our ordinary language use reflects a unified view of ourselves where we do not say "my body is hungry" or "my soul is praying" but we say "I am hungry" and "I am praying." In other words, we experience a unified "I" rather than a separated body and soul. This line of Yeats is particularly resonant with regard to the relation between soul and body because in ancient times the ritual of dance was regarded as an event where people could enter a trance-like or ecstatic experience and thus come into contact with the divine, and the body was symbolized by the dancer. Therefore there are strong suggestions of the union of the spiritual and earthly in this famous line from Yeats. He concludes "Among School Children" with this question, rather than with an answer. Although it may be only a rhetorical question, it could also be a genuine one, the expression of his perplexity, and of his desire to distinguish dancer from dance. In this book, although I recognize how mutually embedded soul and body are, I nevertheless try to tell the dance from the dancer. And perhaps at the end of this exploration we will not be a lot wiser; like Yeats we may still find ourselves at the beginning, "among school children." Indeed we can count ourselves lucky if this journey helps us to re-discover something of the innocence and simplicity of children. Innocence gives children access to the soul. The light of grace can return this access to those who are no longer children and can keep innocence alive with the cooperation of good will, the will that actively goes in search of the good. Simplicity enables children to understand that the strength to become truly great does not come from force or cunning, from talent or brains, but instead is to be found in love. No wonder Jesus encouraged his disciples to learn from little ones. While we may be school children at the end of our quest together, in the sense that there will still be much to learn, at least we will have entered more deeply into the question of the soul.

1

The Living Soul

"...and thus the man became a living soul
[nephesh]. *"*

(Genesis 2:7)

Understanding what the word *nephesh* ("soul") means is not
a straightforward matter. In the Old Testament *nephesh* has
a dizzying variety of meanings. When we come across this
Hebrew word for soul, we instinctively understand it in
terms of our prior understanding of the word "soul". This is
only natural. And our pre-understanding of the word "soul"
is mediated by the culture in which we live. In other words,
the way we understand the term is not something we decide
ourselves. We live in and with a language that others initiated and developed, a language that has been shaped and re-
shaped over a lengthy period by many people. We find ourselves within a horizon of understanding that has been constituted independently of us and without even so much as
consulting us.

Perhaps when we hear the word "soul" it simply evokes
incredulity: in a world where science and physics are so
pervasive and all-explanatory, the soul can seem like an

irrelevance from the bygone past. Maybe the word "soul" encapsulates attitudes and values we want to break free of: a distrust of the body, a narrow-minded and straitjacketed piety that is focused on personal salvation alone, unhappy memories of a disembodied faith that was imposed upon us as children. On the other hand, talk of the soul may hearten us. We may be fed up with soulless living, feeling dislocated and restless in lives devoid of purpose; in such a context, the depth and substance that the soul speaks of may be just the qualities we are yearning for. But whatever the horizon we live in, we can be sure that it is not the same one as that of the world of the Book of Genesis. And we cannot suddenly break free of the historical circumstances in which we are embedded in order to make a romantic and magical leap thousands of years backwards in time in order to get under the skin of the ancient writers of the creation accounts. We cannot realistically unite ourselves with the subjectivity of human beings belonging to such a vastly different cultural and historical context. We live in the twenty-first century and we cannot expect to become contemporaneous with writers of antiquity about whom we know so little.

Yet this inability to enter into a distant life-experience is not necessarily a problem, since our task is not to remove the veils covering the "pure" meaning the composers of the Book of Genesis intended. After all, in the Christian tradition, God is considered as the true author of Scripture, so that the biblical books are written under the inspiration of the Holy Spirit.[10] Our inability to decipher the intentions of the human persons who wrote these texts is therefore a creative opportunity to turn to the divine author, so that with God's help we may tear away the masks in our own world and experience which conceal a hidden and more liberating meaning of the soul from us. Thus, although we cannot be privy to the creative understanding of the persons who composed the creation accounts, it is nevertheless possible "to breathe in" [*inspirare*] something of the richness of these words that are so pregnant with meaning and that have something vital to say about the soul. And if we allow them to do so, these words from so long ago can help us to transcend our present situation in an unexpected manner—not by our springing backwards to a past that can never be retrieved, but by our moving forwards to a new kind of future which these words from God open up for us, a world of new dimensions and freedom which we are invited to inhabit. The resonances in this ancient Hebrew understanding of soul can illuminate our own lives by opening up a new way of understanding the word soul and of living soulfully. Part of that process involves allowing this word *nephesh* to question us, to unsettle the easy certainties we possess so tranquilly, and to comfort our needless unease when it comes to considering the soul.

Most of all, the ancient Hebrew understanding of the word soul can help us to regain a more holistic understanding of the soul, an understanding where body and soul are not separated into two airtight compartments or living uneasily alongside one another like a soon to be divorced couple. This bifurcation is foreign to the Old Testament. The biblical scholar Claus Westermann points out that in our Western Christian culture we often use the pairing "body and soul,"[11] whereas this word pair is never found once in the entire Old Testament.

The Book of Genesis, the first book of the Bible, entitled *Bere'shit* (in the beginning) by the Jews, contains two diverging yet complementary stories of the creation of the human being: one emphasizes God's detachment and sovereign power, the other stresses God's involvement and personal care. These descriptions are like two perspectives on the one event shot from different angles by camera operators who want to focus our attention on different divine qualities. These two accounts, the Yahwist and the Priestly, have different authors from different epochs. The older of the two creation stories, the Yahwist version, possibly dating back to the 10th century BC, is more intimate in nature, unlike the more solemn story in Genesis 1 which reflects, in its authoritative and repetitive tone, the more ritual and cultic concerns of the priestly class. In that priestly account in the first chapter, God seems to be standing outside creation, speaking majestically and transcendently, and once his imperial word sounds, the man and woman come into being.

I will turn to the priestly account in the next chapter. For now let us look at the Yahwist account which reflects a more vivid and emotional sensibility. Rather than the instantaneous creation of the man and woman, there is a steady and unfolding formation of them. The woman is created after the man, and until she is created, the soul of the man is essentially incomplete. God is depicted in an anthropomorphic manner, walking in the Garden of Eden, and even his personal name, *Yahweh*, is added to the more general divine name *Elohim* that we find in the first chapter of Genesis. God is in direct contact with humanity, taking an active part in the shaping of the first human being, a literally "hands-on" role. This Yahwist account clearly shows that the man originates from two different sources. His nature has two distinct elements: dust and breath. He begins as dust and is vivified by the breath of God. This beginning will be echoed in his end when he will exhale his final breath and return to the dust from whence he came (see, for example, Psalm 104:29). God forms and models the man from the dust (*apar*) of the earth, in a manner that evokes a potter lovingly moulding a vase. This image of the potter and vase suggests at once the dependence of the man on God, as well as the man's essential fragility. And once this is done, God, with another gesture that suggests great physical proximity, breathes into his nostrils the breath (*ruach*) of life (Genesis 2:7). The manner in which man is created already distinguishes him from the rest of the animal world. In the account of the creation of animals there is no mention either of them being raised from the dust or of them personally receiving the breath of life from God. Thus the way God creates the human being implicitly points to a new dimension that will not be found among animals. The most noble aspect of this new dimension will be the possibility of a direct and personal relationship with God. The author immediately goes on to declare that it was thus that the man became a living *nephesh*. This Hebrew word *nephesh* is often translated as "being" or "life", but it could also be translated as "soul", because *nephesh* is indeed the Hebrew word for soul. Although each of the animals that God creates has a "living soul" (Genesis 1:30), crucially they do not acquire it through the personal, intimate gesture of God breathing into them.

Genesis 2:7 says nothing about two distinct parts of the human being, namely body and soul. Yet neither does it present the human being as made up of a single stuff or substance. In fact, there is a double origin to the human being, a source that originates in the soil and a principle that is imparted from God. Therefore the human being, although rooted in the clay, also transcends what is earthly. First of all, there is the material origin: the dust of the earth. Interestingly, the word dust (*apar*) is used instead of soil or clay, which are more solid things. Dust presumably indicates the virtual nothingness out of which God raises the human being. And secondly, there is the spiritual origin, denoted by the two extraordinarily intimate gestures of God in fashioning these particles of dust into a man and in breathing the energy that is breath (*ruach*) or life-force into what he has modelled. The origin of the man points to his mission in life: to be faithful to the *adamah* ("earth") from which as *adam* ("man") he emerges, to be rooted in it; and to submit his life to God, to whom he owes the very life he breathes. The dust of the earth and the breath of God are undeniably different. They are not two elements that we would naturally view as congenial or complementary. Yet they combine as an unlikely pair of ingredients to constitute the first human being. Dust is at the margins of matter in the sense that it is made up of particles so minuscule that we can barely see them with the naked eye. In the sunlight we can see specks of dust whirl and rotate through the air; when we shine a lamp on a desk we sometimes notice that the surface is covered by a thin layer of dust. Although we know that dust is everywhere, it remains at the outer edge of our perception. Dust hovers between the frontiers of the visible and the invisible. Not only is dust virtually nothing; furthermore, there is nothing in dust that could enable the human to exist as a human being. Being made of dust unites human beings with everything else rather than distinguishing them, since dust can come from anywhere and anything. If the dust were enough for the human being to operate and function, then the Yahwist account would be proposing a materialist theory. But this is clearly not the case. Even when the dust has been formed and shaped, the human being is still lifeless. Therefore by no legitimate stretch of the imagination can the human being be regarded as a purely material being.

The breath (*ruach*), unlike the dust, is not everywhere. It can arrive suddenly and unexpectedly. Its strength is unpredictable—it may be as gentle as the caress of a summer's breeze or as furious as a tornado. It remains invisible. Interestingly, it is precisely the wind which carries and blows dust everywhere. Without the wind, dust is powerless to move. In an analogical way, the breath or wind that is *ruach* gives the elementary dust a particular direction, one that is ennobling, since the origin of *ruach* is divine. The *ruach* is a kind of life-force that emanates directly from God into the human being, thus making the person alive and capable of performing the functions that are an indispensable part of human existence. Through God's vivifying action the man becomes a living soul. While there are two distinct elements in the human being, dust and wind, these two components are not mirrored in a dual way of functioning. Rather, when it comes to the person's way of existing and being in the world, there is a fundamental and overriding unity. The person is a single and undivided organism.

The man acquires his materiality and shape from the dust which God uses to create him. Therefore it is the dust that is moulded, pressed and kneaded together into man that is the most visible aspect of his being. The breath that God afterwards breathes into his nostrils is an invisible force, despite the fact that this breath makes the man into a living being or living soul. If the matter that makes up human beings according to the Bible is dust, it should not surprise us that we have an enormous amount in common with both inanimate and animate life forms. To a large extent we are physical objects like other physical objects. Contemporary science has discovered that we share an enormous percentage of genes with living forms as varied as bananas (40-50%) and chimpanzees (99%). But the fact that we are genetically so close does not necessarily imply that we are rational and spiritual neighbours. If bananas share almost half of their genes with humans, does that make them at least half human? If chimpanzees share practically all their genes with human beings, how come we have not noticed the budding Mozarts, Michelangelos and da Vincis among our nearest genetic cousins? The reason is because a material or physical description of the human being, while being able for instance to account for 99% of genes common to humans and chimpanzees, cannot account for phenomena such as consciousness and free will.

Despite the enormous advances in contemporary science and genetics, no experimenter has yet managed to produce human beings by selecting the most intelligent chimpanzees or apes and combining them with other highly intelligent animals of their kind. Were this one percentage difference between chimpanzees and humans not so decisive, such a mutation would undoubtedly be possible.

As Genesis shows, despite the enormous material similarity between humans and the dust of the earth, humans are constituted by something in addition, something immaterial and non-physical, expressed in Genesis by the breath or wind that God blows into the nostrils. This rich and invisible inner life of human beings does not show up in genes.

The soul or *nephesh* is the very "aliveness" and vivacity of the body, the principle of personal identity, rather than being an external entity, merely added to the body. The human being as soul is the living creature who experiences the world and who is immersed in the rich world of sensation. Certain of the additional meanings of the word *nephesh* found in the Old Testament are congenial to understanding the word in terms of the concrete life of an individual who lives alongside others, while continuously acknowledging the presence and sovereignty of God. For instance, because the centre of life is the heart, the *nephesh* shows itself in the emotions and affections that connect people. Interestingly enough, the *nephesh* is even used for the physiological hunger (Psalm 107:9) or thirst (Psalm 42:2) that brings us out of ourselves and into contact with the world in order to satisfy such needs. More importantly, the *nephesh* can also stand for hunger and thirst in a deeper sense. The hunger and thirst that yearning for God represents are also denoted by the term *nephesh* (Psalm 63:2). This kind of hunger and thirst differs from literal hunger and thirst because it is not centripetal, directed towards consuming something and reducing it to a part of my metabolism. Physical hunger begins in me, and the object of my hunger returns to me in the form of the food that I chew, swallow and digest. Hunger and thirst for God is centrifugal, because it takes me beyond myself and my limited world. Hunger for God does not find its origin in me; instead I am attracted and drawn by God. And since God is infinite, this hunger can never be satisfied, but only deepened. It continues to be a happy restlessness that is the driving dynamic of the spiritual life. If our souls are alive, they necessarily yearn for God. That is not to say that we all consciously seek God. It is easy to mistake money, power, success, sex, and other things for God so that the energy of our souls gets diverted in the wrong direction. But precisely because these things do not satisfy the uncontainable hunger of our souls, we can hopefully come to know that they are not "the living God" (Psalm 42:2) but ultimately only inert counterfeits.

But *nephesh* is not only used in the Bible with reference to the desire for God; it is also present in human love. The love and friendship between David and Jonathan is characterized by this term in 1 Samuel 18: 1. Jonathan loved David as he loved himself, so much so that they were like one spirit or soul. He defended David's character before his father, and even saved David's life from his father's jealous and envious anger. Although Jonathan was the rightful heir to the throne, he recognized that God had called David to be king. He gave David his royal robe, along with his sword, belt and bow. He freely relinquished his authority over David, pledging himself as his servant. There was no trace of jealousy or envy in this gesture, but only the pure generosity of spirit that rejoiced in the royal destiny of his friend, even though it would mean Jonathan himself could never inherit the throne of his father. This love was full of soul because Jonathan wholeheartedly helped David to fulfil God's purposes rather than trying to bend David to his own.

But in the Old Testament, the word *nephesh* above all means life, especially life as opposed to death. In the Hebrew understanding the *nephesh* is extinguished or breathed out when the person dies, although curiously the word can also be used to designate someone who is dead, as in Numbers 5:2. It is only in the Book of Daniel (12:2) that the idea of resurrection is unambiguously proclaimed. But essentially the emphasis in *nephesh* is on earthly life, one's concrete being here and now that is never a solitary or self-encapsulated existence, but always life with others. This life is a gift from God and is not to be used arbitrarily but as a response to God's gift and in God's service. Responsibility is the way to respond to God's gift of life.

To let this ancient Hebrew understanding of soul speak to us more deeply, we should focus on the larger context in which the word surfaces, rather than looking at the word itself. The description of the man becoming a "living soul" (*nephesh chayah*) is the centre and nexus of the extremely brief Yahwist creation account, that runs from Genesis 2:4b to 2:9. The creation of the man occupies all of one verse, the seventh! Immediately afterwards God sets up the Garden of Eden and places the man within it. The creation of man is not enough; he also needs a living space within which he can flourish. The Garden of Eden is the space where the man who was created is to realize himself and find his fulfilment.

This physically luxurious environment that God gives to the man is of fundamental significance for the meaning of the soul. There is absolutely no hint of a dismissive or hostile attitude to the world to be found in this description. Neither God nor the man spurn or spit upon the Garden of Eden. In order to realize himself, the man needs to enter this world, not to flee it. This umbilical connection between the man and the world is vital. It is especially important to keep this in mind because of our perennial tendency to seek refuge in disincarnate spiritualities. There is something about the high-minded dismissal of the world that attracts the romantic within us. This is probably one reason why a whole generation was captivated by the opening lines of Thomas Merton's compelling autobiography, *The Seven*

Storey Mountain, published a few years after the end of World War II:

> On the last day of January 1915, under the sign of the Water Bearer, in a year of a great war, and down in the shadow of some French mountains on the borders of Spain, I came into the world. Free by nature, in the image of God, I was nevertheless the prisoner of my own violence and my own selfishness, in the image of the world into which I was born. That world was the picture of Hell, full of men like myself, loving God and yet hating Him; born to love Him, living instead in fear and hopeless self-contradictory hungers.[12]

This Trappist monk was so talented a writer that one almost wants to be swept away by his romantic vision that is so contaminated by demonisation of the world and self-loathing. There is something that rouses our spirits at the sight of such a gifted man who found the prospect of a penitential existence in a remote abbey in Kentucky infinitely more rewarding than the glittering academic career that lay invitingly spread out before him. It is only when you turn to Merton's later writings that the excesses of his youthful idealism become unavoidably evident. Not long after he was firmly ensconced in Gethsemane, he began to spend an awful lot of time trying to re-connect with the world he had once so gladly left behind. He wrote poetry, corresponded with artists, took up social activism and Zen meditation. Towards the end of his life he was still lamenting his failure to become the ecstatic self he had passionately described during the bliss that enveloped him while writing *The Seven*

Storey Mountain. And yet his later engagement with the world, rooted as it was in silence and solitude, was more discerning in its evaluation of the good and evil that the world contains.

In any case, God gives the man a world to be enjoyed rather than spat upon. The man has the pleasure of looking and walking around a beautiful garden, of eating the fruit from the trees, of inhaling the pure air. The earth he walks on is watered by underground springs and a river that gushes forth from the soil. There is no need to plant any crops because all that he needs for food is already blossoming in front of his eyes. Yet the creation of the man is not purely for enjoyment. God gives him both a task of work and an ethical responsibility. The man's task (Genesis 2:15) is to act as steward and caretaker of the garden, overseeing the flourishing life before him. This work that is rooted in the soil is evidently not regarded as degrading, since it forms an integral part of the paradisiacal condition of the first man. In some ways the garden is a guardian of the man, nourishing and sustaining him, keeping him alive: already in bloom, its maintenance does not require a lot of effort on his part. Although the man is above the earth in the hierarchy of values, God's command is clearly to tend it and cultivate it in a manner that enhances it rather than to exploit it in a way that leads to its destruction. In fact, because of his origin in the dust of the earth, the man's life is inextricably bound up with the soil and to abuse the land would be a betrayal of the primeval bond that ties him to it, as well as being an affront to the God who has created both the earth and himself from it. By remaining faithful to God's command, this world that he tends will also cultivate him, furthering the process of creation that first begun with God's direct action.

As well as being given a working task, the man is also entrusted with moral responsibility (Genesis 2:17), inasmuch as he is commanded by God not to eat from the tree of knowledge of good and evil. Ethics always presupposes a relationship, in this case a relationship between the man and God. The relationship calls the man to responsibility in his actions. Given the fact that God forbids him to eat only from one tree, but allows him to eat from every other one, this ordinance is not demanding or exacting. Yet the sanction for disobeying this order is of the utmost seriousness: if the man eats from this tree, he will die. Once again, this highlights and reinforces the reality of the man's dependence upon God for his life. Yet it is also a profound acknowledgement of the freedom of man, a freedom which characterizes somebody with a soul. This freedom of the man is not unlimited. He evidently did not choose to be born, nor the place in which he finds himself, the body he has been given, and so on. But he can choose how he is going to exist within the parameters of his circumstances and context. Now freedom does not have much meaning if it does not entail the freedom to do wrong. God does not control the man's actions, he does not force him to act in a particular way. He presents the man with the freedom to choose. Ultimately, the man can order his actions as he sees fit. He is not constrained to choose a particular course of action. He is free to define the kind of person he wants to be: obedient to God or a rebel against God's law. The choice is up to him.

Despite the idyllic nature of the environment in which he finds himself, despite the earthly task and moral responsibility with which he has been entrusted, his soul and selfhood have not yet emerged fully. The natural and even animal worlds are not sufficient for the man. The sense of personal identity that is the soul does not abide in isolation. And yet not any kind of company is sufficient. It is human companionship that the man yearns for. The renowned Greek philosopher Aristotle (384–322 BC) was later to comment that no human being would freely choose to live without friends, even though possessing every other good thing.[13] But there has been a tendency in the Christian tradition to view human company as an impediment to the life of the soul. Take for instance the famous medieval Christian work of devotion, *The Imitation of Christ*, arguably a book that next to the Bible has had the greatest influence on Christians. In Book One, Chapter 20, which is devoted to the love of silence and solitude, the author approvingly quotes someone who asserted that as often as he had been among men, he had returned less a man. This is manifestly not the mindset that informs the vision of the soul we find in Genesis.

The environment the man inhabits is much more expansive than a medieval monastic cell, yet even in this stunning setting he does not feel fully human. God creates a splendid garden for him, and then brings him all of animal life so that the man might give each creature a name. Despite this invitation to co-operate in God's creative activity, the man still feels a fundamental lack, for no companion or helper has been found who can be his equal, who corresponds to him in worth and dignity. This sense of lack is an indication that the man is more than simply a body. It is likely that the man became painfully aware of this lack as he was naming the animals that God brought before him, possibly because these animals came before him in pairs. Seeing that each male animal had a female companion, the man must have

41

longed for a female companion for himself. It was also clear to the man that none of these animals could be his equal. Certainly in one sense they were creatures like himself, but in another sense he found them wanting. The man had the gift of language, since he was able to give names to the animals. But they could not speak back to him. They could not communicate on his level. Neither could they satisfy the hunger of his living soul. The man had "soul" enough not only to recognize the animals as animals and to be able to give them names, but also to realize he was qualitatively different from them. God, who could read his thoughts and discern his hunger for a companion, sent the man into a deep sleep. During sleep, consciousness and will are totally or at least partially suspended and the person's interaction with the surrounding environment ceases. Ancient Egyptian thought regarded sleep as a temporary death which was nevertheless restorative and creative. In the case of the man, this state of rest is a fount of life in an unexpected way, as God creates woman from his side.

The woman adds a new dimension to the man's soul; in fact, she seems to surpass him spiritually. This fact is not self-evident. Indeed the account of the creation of woman can easily be interpreted as a justification for the subordination of woman. However, it can also be seen in a kinder light. Admittedly the Hebrew word *ezer*, which means "helper" can be dismissed as a term that demeans woman, but this would make it all the more puzzling why it is applied to God in several books of the Old Testament (e.g. Exodus 18:4, Deuteronomy 33:7, Psalm 33:20, etc.). If God, who is superior to human beings, can be described as a helper of Israel, this implies that the description of the woman as a helper does not necessarily imply that she is inferior to the man. Moreover, although God created man from the insignificance of dust, he creates woman from a more noble source: from the side of man, in other words from the side of a creature who has dominion over creation and to whom has been imparted the life-giving breath of God. If the man, who emerges from the dust, can be such a sophisticated creature, the woman who emerged from the man after he has been polished and refined by God must be even more so. Perhaps it was the side where the heart is located, because the woman was the one who brought the man out of himself, teaching him to love. Furthermore, although the woman derived from the man's side, the man himself had no say in her creation. God created her in *his* divine way while the man was asleep. Although the man knew that he lacked something, he did not know exactly what he needed to complete himself. The woman is not man's invention but God's creation and God's free and undreamt of gift. And if the relation between the chronology of God's creation of the world and the relative importance of what he creates is anything to go by, then the movement is upwards from the most basic, i.e. inanimate manner, to the most advanced, i.e. the human being. If that logic holds, then the woman, not the man (since she is the final creature to be created), is the crown of creation.

God brings the woman before the man (Genesis 2:22). Although God had shown the animals to the man, they had not met with anything like the reaction that the woman's appearance evinces from him. The marvel of the woman's creation meets with the man's immediate and ecstatic approval as soon as he awakes from his slumber: "This is now bone of my bones, and flesh of my flesh" (Genesis 2:23). Only now, in this spontaneous outburst of praise and jubilation, is his creation complete. It is through the woman that the man comes into full possession of life and of his soul. It is in this interpersonal relationship that his personality finds its completion. The full implications of God's statement that it is not good for the man to be alone (Genesis 2:18) become evident in this happy surprise.

The love of the woman raises the man up to a higher sphere, much as Johann Wolfgang von Goethe (1749-1832) describes *das Ewig-Weibliche* ("the Eternal Feminine") as drawing us ever upwards in the final lines of Part 2 of Faust, one of the greatest plays ever written. Although Goethe's lyrical expression can be dismissed as dreamy and over-effusive, it does express a truth about the goodness, affection, lightness of touch and beauty that are unique to women. It is not only in Goethe that one finds this cherishing of the feminine. The exaltation of the all-redeeming feminine is also a feature of the Romantic movement. Admittedly Romanticism can be interminably solipsistic and nauseatingly sentimental, but at its best it is sublimely imaginative, visionary and original. Romanticism dramatizes in an unrestrained manner this truth about the woman and her effect on the man that is already present in Genesis. Friedrich Schiller (1759-1805), the towering German dramatist and poet of the second half of the eighteenth century, spoke of *die schöne Seele* ("the beautiful soul") in ways that faintly echo the effect the first woman presumably had upon the first man. For Schiller the beautiful soul has an inner beauty that unself-consciously radiates an irresistible grace even when perfect physical beauty is wanting. The beautiful soul is a pure spirit, without guise. This type of personality reconciles the opposites of heart and head, duty and inclination, into a stunningly harmonious whole.

The grace of the first woman's beautiful soul embellished the soul of the first man.

In the aftermath of the Fall, the body is doomed to death. However, there is no sign that the soul will die; it remains immortal. In order to put this truth in context, let us look at the different aspects of the punishment imposed by God. It is almost more true to say that the punishment is not imposed by God but unfolds logically from the nature of the first couple's sin. Thousands of years later in Dante's *Inferno* we find an echo of this, where the punishment suffered by the inhabitants of hell fits their sins with uncanny accuracy. The hypocrites, for instance, walk around a small area in beautifully adorned monastic robes which are in fact leaden, so that the despite this deceptively attractive and holy exterior, they are in fact forced to bear the crippling burden of their hypocrisy and deceit for all eternity. After the man and woman have disobeyed God by eating of the fruit of the tree, the woman, who had been sure of finding joy and freedom in her relationship with the man and in bearing children, is now condemned to finding pain and subjection there. Although the man and woman will continue to have a relationship, it will no longer bring with it the idyllic rapport they previously enjoyed. This turbulent relationship will be especially hard on the woman. "To the woman he said, 'I will intensify the pains of childbirth; in pain you shall give birth to children. Your desire shall be for your husband, and he shall be your master'" (Genesis 3:16).

As for the man, because he listened to the voice of the woman rather than obeying the command of God, he will now experience his work in a negative way. Previously he had enjoyed his labour, now it will become burdensome and drain his energy. Because he ate of the forbidden fruit, he will now find that everything edible comes at the price of great personal struggle and travail. The ground that was once fertile will now be barren, the fruit that was so copious will now be scarce. Most ominously he is told of the certainty of death: "for you are dust and unto dust you shall return" (Genesis 3:19). Without God, the man will crumble into the virtual nothingness from which he originally came: dust. This is not simply physical death; it is also the death that separation from communion with God brings in its wake.

However, despite the bleakness of the human scenario, there is encouraging news. God does not take back the vivifying breath of life that he has personally given to the man. Were God considering the complete destruction of human beings, he would have not only consigned them to dust, but also taken away the *ruach*, which is precisely what made the man a living soul or being in Genesis 2:7. Despite the disobedience of the first couple, God does not renege on mankind. This is already an indication that even with the advent of death, there may be life afterwards: for if God does not take away the enlivening breath or wind he has given, the human being will not disappear after death.

2

Image and Likeness

"God created human beings in his image."
(Genesis 1:27)

The second account of the creation of the human being, which is presented in the first chapter of Genesis, while not using the word soul, can nevertheless tell us a lot about it. This is because being made in the image and likeness of God confers an extraordinary dignity on the human being that is reflected in the whole person. In this priestly narrative, the human being is created on the sixth day, as the culminating point of God's creation (Genesis 1:26ff). The special nature of the creation of the human being is already indicated by significant points of difference from the other days, despite an overall structural similarity. In the previous five days, God speaks tersely and solemnly, saying simply "let there be" and immediately we are told "and there was". However, when it comes to human creation, God unexpectedly uses the first person plural, "let us make" (Genesis 1:26). Was this the expression of an internal dialogue? Was he using the royal "we"? Did the author have a sense, however inchoate, of a plurality within God? There is not enough data available to decipher the intentions of the writer. Therefore, instead of engaging in an archaeological bid to dig up a lost and irrecoverable meaning, I propose to read into these words the teleological anticipation of a meaning that was not yet in the possession of the priestly author of Genesis. Despite the fact that the person writing these words was clearly bereft of any concept of the Trinity, I already hear in this phrase a distant prophecy of the Trinity, as early Christian thinkers did.

The crux of verse 26 is the declaration that the human being will be made "in our image and after our likeness." A lot of ink has been spilled trying to unravel the possible meanings of this phrase. In one sense such a lot of spilled ink seems unnecessary, since the fact that we live in such an image-saturated world should furnish us with a distinct advantage when it comes to understanding images. After all, they are omnipresent. Images have become so powerful, through mass media and information technology, that they often drown out words. In politics image is, ironically, threatening to become the real "substance" in election campaigns. While celebrities are intent on protecting their image rights, minor stars and even ordinary people get makeovers and plastic surgery. Teenage girls internalize the ideal body that advertisers present. But though this glut of images provides never-ending stimulus and continual sensationalism, it also removes us from the realities of commitment and the nuances of feeling, making our lives shallower and cheapening our sense of the good, the true and the beautiful. Speaking of the role of the image in postmodern culture, Richard Kearney remarks:

No more is it a question of images representing some transcendent reality, as tradition had it. The very notion of such a reality is now unmasked as an illusionist effect. The wheel has turned full circle. But the mirror of the postmodern paradigm reflects neither the outer world of nature nor the inner world of subjectivity; it reflects only itself—a mirror within a mirror within a mirror . . .[14]

Because images today often lack a sense of depth and mystery, they no longer seem to participate in the realities they represent. They come across as mass-produced, empty and impersonal copies. In fact, rather than drawing our attention to the originals of which they are copies, they often divert attention to themselves. Their superficiality corresponds with the shallowness we often sense in our Western culture. However, because we are bombarded so relentlessly with these empty images, their sheer quantity acts as an anaesthetic, numbing our ability to imagine or conjure up alternative images that are suffused with originality and reality.

Although we need to go beyond the depersonalization of pseudo-images, to appreciate more deeply the fact that the human being is in the image and likeness of God, we must also beware of confusing or conflating the image with the original. In other words, despite being in the image and likeness of God, the human being is certainly not God. According to Genesis the human being resembles God, rather than sharing in the divine nature. While human beings are definitely not divine, they are certainly royalty. Neighbouring cultures reserved for kings the prerogative of being images of God. It was subversive and revolutionary to declare that all human beings were images of God. This is what the priestly author of Genesis did by implicitly declaring that all humanity was kingly.

The Hebrew words *tselem* (image) and *demuth* (likeness), despite their different nuances, are fundamentally similar. Indeed, even in our everyday speech today, image and likeness are closely connected. In fact, an image normally comes under the category of a likeness, since most images (abstract art being a notable exception!) are also likenesses. In the Bible, each term is used in both concrete and abstract senses. Since these terms are so close as to be often interchangeable in practice, it may be that by using both, the writer simply wanted to highlight the wonderfully radical truth of what he was saying. The human being is like God. Since the priestly writer does not divorce body from soul, it would seem that it is the whole person that is similar to God. In other words, it is not only personality, intelligence, and freedom that resemble God but also physical appearance. However, the latter form of resemblance is contestable, given that God is an incorporeal being, a pure spirit. How can a human being in his or her external appearance be like God who is invisible? The image and likeness of God that human beings are endowed with could alternatively refer to their function in the world. The function of an image is to represent as faithfully as possible the original of which it is a copy. Ideally the human being should be a mirror without blemish pointing towards God. In order to be an effective mirror, the human being needs to reflect God who is primary, rather than being a self-reflecting mirror.

Before God actually creates the first human being, he describes the function of this highest of creatures in Genesis 1:26, by proclaiming that the human being is to exercise dominion over the fish of the sea, the birds of the air, the cattle, the reptiles and the whole earth. Interestingly, God excludes the lights of the heaven from the dominion of humankind. The stars, sun and moon have themselves been given authority by God—it is their role, and not that of human beings, to rule the day and the night as well as to divide light from darkness (Genesis 1:14-18). Therefore the human being is not above the stars, a fact which is confirmed by Psalm 8. "When I consider your heavens, the work of your fingers, the moon and the stars, which you have set in place, what are human beings that you are mindful of them, mortals that you care for them? Yet you have made them a little lower than the heavenly beings and crowned them with glory and honour." (Psalm 8:3-5) According to the priestly story of creation, the sphere of the universe outside of our planet is beyond our ken. Modern science offers an intriguing postscript on the importance assigned to the stars in Genesis. Although we imagine that the stars are solely *outside* of us—after all, we look up at the stars in the night sky—science has shown us that the stars are also *inside* of us, in the sense that practically all the atoms of our bodies were produced and formed inside stars. We are star material.

In order to become more aware of the extraordinary gift that being made in the image of God entails, it is helpful to look at the reverse process for a moment: how we "make" God in our image and likeness. This making is obviously not literal: it occurs in the imagination. We do not necessarily imagine God as a personal copy of ourselves; more often we envisage him as resembling some significant person in our experience. For instance, God can be a kind old man with a white beard, a stern schoolteacher, a warm mother, an exacting father, and so on. Although at the level of language we proclaim a belief in the God of love, we may simultaneously harbour a different image in our minds. What we proclaim at the level of dogma may be abstract and impersonal, having little impact on our lives, whereas the image of God that we mentally see is always concrete and often charged with emotion, shaping our lives in a fateful manner. If our image of God is deficient in some way, it is generally the case that our self-image, God-relationship and way of life are correspondingly lacking. For instance, if we see God as an angry prison warden, we are likely be afraid of him, to see ourselves as bad people who deserve to be punished and locked up, and to act out of that self-understanding. Despite the fact that our image of God only exists in the imagination, it can have crucial consequences on our relationship with God, on our own self-image as well as on our moral behaviour.

If our image of God can be so decisive in shaping our lives, then the fact that God not only imagined us in his image but created us in fidelity to this image is truly momentous in terms of what it means for God and for us. It means absolute commitment on his part to what he has made, for God would never be disloyal to himself or to any creature, not to mention one who is so much like him. The extraordinary lengths to which God's faithful love extend become obvious in his response to the Fall—sending his Son into the world in order to demonstrate this love in all its infinite extent. It means for our part that, being made in God's image, we entertain unsuspected depths, that we are much vaster than we can either dream or imagine.

In Genesis 1:27 the act of creating human beings is described with a triple repetition of the word *bara*, "to create".

This may refer back to the "let us make" of the previous verse. Again reading into the text from a Christian point of view, rather than reading out of it as scriptural scholars do, this threefold use of the word *bara* could be regarded as a discreet albeit unintentional sign of the Trinity. The verse goes on to say that God created human beings "masculine and feminine." The priestly author seems to give a more privileged role to the woman than is found in the second chapter of Genesis, since there is no mention of her being created after the man (though as I have argued in Chapter 1, her later arrival is not necessarily a sign of her lesser importance). But this emphasis on the masculine and feminine pole of humanity does complement the Yahwist author's account, since it points to the fundamental incompleteness of either man or woman alone. In order to be the image of God, a human being cannot be isolated but must exist in community.

In Genesis 1:28, God gives his blessing to the couple, wishing them fruitfulness in their relationship with one another and success in their dominion over the earth. In the following verse, God inaugurates a vegetarian diet, announcing that the "meat" of the first human beings is to be fruits, herbs, etc., from plant life. No living being is to be killed in order to sustain the life of human beings, because there is a more peaceful way of surviving and blossoming. This is also the rule for animals. They are not to kill other animals but to consume plants. Thus the dominion of the earth by human beings has strict parameters. The earth, as God's creation, is intrinsically valuable, and human beings have no right to undermine that value. God's goodness is so expansive that he created myriad creatures; and unfortunately, by harming these creatures or causing their extinction, we are implicitly slighting God.

The benign vegetarian regime eventually fell apart when human beings ceased being sacred stewards and became exploitative masters. But the prophets associate its return with an eschatological period of harmony, as for instance in Isaiah's prediction of a messianic reign of peace in which the wolf and the lamb will peacefully coexist (Isaiah 11:6). The wisdom of revering the lives of animals has once again become evident today as natural resources dwindle at an alarming rate and human obesity reaches gargantuan proportions.

Having concluded the creation of the world with the creation of humanity, God concludes that it is *very* good, thus indicating his especial pleasure. Living as they do in harmony with God, the man and the woman enter into the seventh day, the first full day of their existence, not with the task of working, but in order to share in the joyful rest of the *Shabbat* ("to cease, to rest") that God has instituted, a discreet sign of God's caring love. Since they are created in God's image and likeness, they are called to emulate the Creator by desisting from activity on that day. By not working on this first day, the man and woman offer the beginning of their lives to God, acknowledging his lordship and witnessing to the fact that the world around them is not theirs, but belongs to the Creator. The fact that their lives are fully launched on this day of rest is also an invitation by God to begin nobly, in order to strengthen their resolve to continue likewise; in other words, not immediately to dominate the earth but to learn how to reverence it first through contemplation so that their stewardship will be life-giving. They have the opportunity to ponder the fact that the authority they have over the earth is a sacred gift instead of a natural right.

This day of rest is a "soul time" because it offers the man and woman the opportunity to strengthen the bond of love that unites them with each other and with God. It is not merely an empty interlude that precedes the business of real living. On the contrary, it is the summit of existence because it expresses what life is all about. It is a time when they are not taken up in work but can immerse themselves in the divine. It is also a day when they are not stewards of the world but custodians of their hearts. It is a day when they can stop to consider God's image within themselves and beautify it. This is above all God's day. In the six previous days, the man and woman had done nothing, since they had only come into existence on the sixth day. It was God who had done all the work. And now is their chance to rejoice with him and to relish his handiwork, to get in touch with the mystery of his beauty above them, around them, and within them.

The priestly narrative shows that God does not create only a spiritual being; he creates a whole person. Although the first man and woman are dependent upon God because they are created by God, they are simultaneously elevated above the created world (although they do not transcend the lights of the heaven). However, the fact that they are made in the image and likeness of God does not so much impart information about their nature as about their function. They are given the task of representing God and ruling on God's behalf, not for their own purposes.

Although they transcend the world by virtue of being in God's image, they are also immanent to it. They are both beyond the world and within it. An extremely dualistic conception of spirit and matter would lead to an emphasis on transcendence at the expense of immanence. What Genesis teaches opposes certain strong currents in Christian spirituality: in other words, Genesis teaches that we have to be on earth, and rooted in nature, to find freedom and fulfilment. It is through arriving in the world of nature (and not departing from it) that the great adventure of life begins for the first human beings. Although with Abraham the motif of homelessness and pilgrimage began, at this stage in Genesis human beings are robustly inserted into the world. This planet is neither a prison nor a cosmic outpost for them: it is their home.

Genesis teaches us to recover our continuity with the universe. This is not a matter of denying that we have souls. Instead it is a matter of avoiding the hubris involved in repudiating that we are also bodies. Therefore a dual perspective on the human being is necessary. The human being is still part of the world and cannot just use the world in any way he or she wants. Crucially, the whole universe, and not just the human being, is "charged with the grandeur of God" (Gerard Manley Hopkins). This is because God is both above creation (transcendent) and also present and active in it (immanent). God is present wherever there is life, and the animal or inanimate world cannot be simply regarded as devoid of divine presence and therefore exploitable. The natural world is not simply an empty stage-set, bereft of God. Nature is the privileged setting in which God creates human beings and reveals himself to them. It is the embracing horizon within which God fashions the human being, and therefore in which God will continue to shape the human being. Unfortunately we have thrown nature out of theology, and sometimes our own nature as well. We have falsely deduced superiority because we discovered we were different from the rest of creation, leading us to act aloofly.

In all of the priestly presentation of the creation of humanity, there is no sense of the soul as separate. It is woven seamlessly into the rich tapestry of life that God inaugurates. However, as we will see from considering further scriptural passages from the Old Testament, this seamless fabric is nevertheless woven—in other words, although the soul forms a whole with the body, it can nevertheless be distinguished in a meaningful way from the corporeal element. For the Old Testament makes it clear that human beings survive death. Generally this is in a languid and diminished state. They are consigned to the unprepossessing surroundings of Sheol, where life is anything but varied and dramatic. Some part of them continues to exist in that netherworld. Thus the image and likeness of God that is bequeathed to human beings is not lost with time, but is a permanent gift, even though in Sheol the image becomes paler and more ghostly. But Sheol is not always the ultimate destination, for there are eventually even clear intimations of resurrection in the Old Testament. This resurrection also brings the body to new life.

Before we go further, it is again important to beware of importing contemporary perspectives on image and likeness into our understanding of the human being as described in Genesis and the Old Testament. In his celebrated essay from 1936, entitled "The Work of Art in the Age of Mechanical Reproduction", Walter Benjamin sounded the alarm about the dire cultural consequences of the universal accessibility of art as a result of the latter's reproducibility. He was convinced that the uniqueness, aura and quality of presence of works of art were lost through mass reproduction. Today he would no doubt become apoplectic at the overwhelming flood of cheap images that can be downloaded in seconds with a single personal computer.

Although we are surrounded today by more images than ever before, we also consider them as less real. Of course, images were never regarded as fully sharing in the reality they represented. But they were considered to have a substantial, if limited, participation in the original that they portrayed. Because of this weight of reality accruing to images, the Old Testament was adamant in its prohibition of representations of God (a fact which throws into relief the extraordinary risk involved in God's gesture of freely creating humanity in his image and likeness). The Old Testament does not regard the human being as a disposable commodity, as temporary or replaceable. The divine image in human beings is so substantial that it is not only lasting but immortal, in imitation of the supreme original of which it is a resemblance. Although this image is disfigured by the Fall, it is not destroyed, as is evident from Genesis 9:6: "If anyone sheds the blood of a human being, by a human shall that person's blood be shed; for God made humankind in his own image."

According to the Old Testament, people do not cease to exist after death, though they do cease to exist in the manner in which they existed while on earth. The Hebrew word that is used for the dead is *rephaim*. Apparently this word comes from *rapheh*, which denotes powerlessness, weakness or even a shade or shadow. All of the dead, irrespective of their national origin, religious beliefs or moral character, end up in a place called *Sheol*. Enoch and Elijah are the only exceptions: they are directly taken up into heaven (see Genesis 5:24 and 2 Kings 2:11). Sheol, the lowest level of the Hebrew universe, is sometimes described as a deep cavernous pit under the earth. This realm of the dead is a place of abandonment (Psalm 88:4-5). The inhabitants of Sheol can no longer count upon God's fidelity (Isaiah 38:18). Grim as it may be, the netherworld is not a place of torture but simply spectral and phantom-like as one might expect of an insubstantial spirit world. Because the prospect of being consigned to Sheol is distinctly unpalatable, long lives with plentiful offspring are welcomed both as a reward for righteousness and as an opportunity to defer the inevitable as long as possible.

The dead do not bring their bodies with them to Sheol. Their flesh and bones go to the grave. In other words, continued human existence after death is possible without a body. Therefore the human being is a composite made up of different parts. While that much is clear, it is not evident what dimension of humans endures in this dreary afterlife. In general the Old Testament presents a minimalist portrait of the level and quality of existence that are possible in Sheol. For the most part, it is an inactive existence. This is perhaps because the body is so important in Hebrew thought that the writers of the Old Testament could not conceive of a full or adequate existence in its absence. Indeed they recoiled in horror at the very idea of an existence without a body. A soul that continued to be in the absence of a body not only fell terribly short of reality for the Hebrew mind but was also a possibility they abhorred. Whereas in Greek thinkers such as Plato, the soul tends to be the real person and the body is tolerated despite being a frequent obstacle to self-realization, in ancient Hebrew anthropology a person cannot be fulfilled without an incarnate existence that enables him or her to relish and enjoy the riches of this life and of this earth.

However, Old Testament eschatology is not exhausted by Sheol, for this spectral dwelling in the subterranean recesses of the earth is not the final word about the afterlife. There is also the belief that God has something better in store than sleepy oblivion. Psalm 16:10 confidently proclaims that God will not abandon the Psalmist to the grave nor let his loved one know decay. Psalm 49:15 is adamant that God will rescue the psalmist from the shadowy realm of Sheol. The new possibility entertained here is not a subdued state of partial animation but a full and pulsating life of communion with God. The Book of Job seems to speak strongly of resurrection: "After my skin has been destroyed, I will see God in my flesh". (Job 19:26). However some scholars suggest that the destruction of Job's skin may refer to his awful illness rather than to his death; they also point out that the phrase "in my flesh" could also be translated as "without my flesh".

Most startling of all is the awesome proclamation in Isaiah 26:19—"Your dead will live; their corpses will rise. You who lie in the dust, awake and shout for joy, for your dew is as the dew of the dawn, and the earth will give birth to the departed spirits." This verse implies that Sheol is a provisional state of inactive and comatose existence after death, which is then superseded by resurrection, at which moment corpses will come to life again. In the original Hebrew the term for "departed spirits" is the *rephaim*, confirming that the shady existence of the dead is temporary, not permanent. The departed spirits will be united with the bodies they have left behind so that the whole person enters into new life. Although this passage from Isaiah is an isolated one, it seems unambiguous about the resurrection.

Possibly reflecting the exposure to other cultures and currents of thought during the Jewish exile, The Book of Daniel clearly refers to a general resurrection. In this apocalyptic book which reflects a period of enormous tension and upheaval in Jewish history, the promise of resurrection from the dead must have sounded like a tremendous consolation (except for those who would be resurrected to everlasting contempt): "Many of those who sleep in the dust of the earth will awake, some to everlasting life, some to shame and everlasting disgrace. Those who are wise shall shine brightly like the splendour of the firmament, and those who lead many to righteousness, like the stars forever and ever" (Daniel 12:2-3).

Death veils the question of the soul's immortality in darkness. Faith promises to unveil the answer and to illuminate the darkness of the shadow cast by death: the soul, this principle in the human being by which he or she wills, thinks and feels, and which animates the body, is not destined to end with death. If these vital functions of volition, intelligence, feeling and so on are to survive death, it must be by a special intervention of God, since the body which enables the soul to function will at least for a time no longer exist. That God might intervene in this way makes thorough sense, since "God is not the God of the dead, but of the living" (Luke 20:38).

3

The Immortal Soul

"This Jack, joke, poor potsherd, 'patch,
matchwood, immortal diamond,
Is immortal diamond."
Gerard Manley Hopkins, "That Nature is a Heraclitean Fire
and of the Comfort of the Resurrection"

The question of the immortality of the soul started fading out of theological sight from the middle of the twentieth century. This waning of interest in the soul's immortality coincided with a debate about its unbiblical nature, as well as a developing interest in political and liberation theologies. In his celebrated 1955 Ingersoll Lecture at Harvard University, later published as *Immortality of the Soul or Resurrection of the Dead? The Witness of the New Testament* (London: The Epworth Press, 1958), Oscar Cullmann contrasted the death of Socrates and the death of Jesus. According to Cullmann, because of Socrates' belief in the immortality of the soul, he was convinced that his soul would not die, but live on, and so he looked forward to death as a release from the body. For Jesus, however, death was not serene but frightening, since it entailed the destruction of the life created by God. If immortality of the soul (as in Socrates) is about continuation of the same, resurrection (as in Cullmann) is about a new creation, the bringing back to life of the whole person who has truly died. Cullmann concluded that if the soul is immortal then resurrection is unnecessary, whereas if we are to believe in the Resurrection we cannot simultaneously adhere to immortality of the soul. There must be a resurrection for both body and soul.

Although Cullmann's distinction is illuminating in some respects, it is also somewhat of a simplification, a fact which he himself recognized and which is why he qualified and nuanced this initial contrast in the course of his lecture. For instance, Cullmann granted that the Bible never talks of complete death in the sense of annihilation. Cullmann also pointed out that the New Testament shows that the Early Church comes close to the Greek teaching on the immortality of the soul.[15]

Karl Barth was another critic of the doctrine of the immortality of the soul:

> Man as such, however, belongs to this world. He is thus finite and mortal. One day he will only have been, as once he was not. His divinely given promise and hope and confidence in this confrontation with God is that even as this one who has been he will share the eternal life of God Himself. Its content is not, therefore, his liberation from his this-sidedness, from his end and dying, but positively the glorification by the eternal God of his natural and lawful this-sided, finite, and mortal being.[16]

In the 1960s theologians such as Johannes Baptist Metz, influenced among other sources by the faithless hope of the Marxist philosopher Ernst Bloch, turned their attention away from immortality of the soul and focused instead on a this-worldly eschatology, a hope for the here and now through the transformation of politics, economics and society. Liberation theologians of the 1970s and 1980s, while not dismissing issues such as the soul, concentrated instead on developing a theology that could help transform the destinies of the oppressed. For instance, in his seminal study *Theology of Liberation* (first published in Spanish in 1971) Gustavo Gutierrez devotes his attention to liberation in the here and now.

While all these developments in theology enriched our understanding of the Bible as well as making us more aware of the urgent imperative to engage in social and political praxis, we have lost something of reality in the process as well. In fact, the most real thing of all has somehow been veiled, although not totally occluded, by imminent eschatologies—and that thing is death. The dialectical theology of Barth is no longer in fashion, the political theology of Metz may seem dated, even the theologies of liberation are no longer the talking point they once were, but one thing is certain—death is not going away. Each of us can be sure of two things—I am going to die, and my death is getting closer each day. Death is not simply something that befalls other people. The brute and unpalatable truth is that I too am going to die. And not just on some indeterminate day, but at a particular day and at a specific time.

Although the fact of death has been upsetting us for thousands of years, humanity has also been trying to minimize it for millennia. Epicurus (341-270 BC), came up with the famous maxim "if you are, death is not; if death is, you are not" in his *Letter to Menoeceus*, using this, among other things, to argue against the fear of death. However, the facts are not as clear-cut as Epicurus suggests. After all, at the moment of death, we are still alive, since we cannot be already dead if we are passing from life to death. Therefore, there is a moment when death is and we are as well, however tenuous our hold on existence is, and that alone is frightening. Of course it is also true that once that moment has gone by and we have passed from life into death, we are no longer alive.

But once we are dead, Epicurus' argument seems more convincing, at least if we accept his premise that with death the self no longer exists. For if the self no longer is, there is no longer a self to suffer harm or to experience pain, and so there is nothing to fear in death. However, even before we appeal to the Christian belief in an afterlife, we can find shortcomings in Epicurus' argument. Thomas Nagel, for instance, has provided a telling counterargument to Epicurus.[17] He invites us to engage in a thought experiment, imagining an intelligent person who is reduced to the state of a contented infant because of a brain injury. Although this person does not experience any harm and indeed remains content thanks to excellent nursing care, *we* nevertheless look on this brain injury as a tragedy and a serious blow. It is not that there is anything bad about being a cheerful infant. What is bad is the fact that the person has lost wonderful gifts as well as the future. In an analogous way, death is bad because of what it takes away from those who die. It deprives them of the good things they have and it also deprives them of the possibility of realizing the talents and gifts they have.

Whatever we may think about his conclusions, at least Epicurus had the courage to think about death. Other thinkers have preferred to sidestep it altogether. In a letter to the aristocratic and unconventional Madame du Deffand, written on 18 November 1761, Voltaire advised her never to think of death. He was convinced such a thought could only poison life. Instead he recommended living from day to day. Contemporary Western culture tends to concur with Voltaire. Death has become less present for a variety of reasons: many people die out of sight in hospital rather than in the visibility of their homes; because of the drop in infant mortality and the rise in life expectancy the majority of those who die are elderly; cremation burns away the most graphic sign of death, the corpse; the process of grieving is limited in scope to family and friends and confined in time to a few hours off work; we now have successful treatments for so many illnesses that were once automatically terminal (e.g. diabetes, heart conditions, different forms of cancer, etc.) that many of us forget that these wonderful advances do not eliminate death, but only delay its advent. Even though the mass media saturates us with images of murder, war and disasters, these virtually present deaths tend to desensitize us to the real thing. We notice that Western countries devote significant resources to medical research and crime prevention; we tend to forget how this is eclipsed by the huge budgets spent on weapons of destruction. But for all that, death still gnaws away at us. Because our culture is more individualist in nature and focused on the quest for personal fulfilment and self-realization, death is perceived as a more tragic loss than ever before, since it deprives the individual of life and fulfilment.

There are thinkers who focus our thoughts on death. The twentieth century philosopher, Martin Heidegger (1889-1976), was convinced there was much to be said about how to face this unavoidable aspect of human existence and come to terms with it. Unlike Voltaire, Heidegger believed that we should not ignore our finiteness. By becoming aware of my being-towards-death and appropriating this experience of my impending nothingness, I can reach a deeper level of existence than the surface conformity of the crowd.

Heidegger's discussion of death contrasts with that of the Jewish thinker Emmanuel Levinas (1906-1995), whose own thinking about death is a thinly veiled rebuke directed at Heidegger's thought. But to be fair to Heidegger, it is worth pointing out that Levinas and Heidegger are essentially talking of two different issues: Levinas is discussing the reaction of the person to the imminence of death, in a manner that evokes Dostoevsky's account of his own near experience of almost certain death. Heidegger is interested in how the realization of death's inevitability can touch the kind of reflective person for whom death instinctively seems light-years away; in other words, what can facing up to the fact of death do for a thoughtful person in the here and now? For Levinas, death is distinguished above all by its alterity—its otherness: "something whose very existence is made of alterity."[18] It is so "other" than I cannot make any sense of it. For Heidegger, on the other hand, "death is in every case mine;"[19] it is my possession. Because I can reflect on its advent, I can interiorise the fact that I am going to die. Moreover, in Heidegger's view, the prospect of death engenders lucidity and virility. It throws a light on my existence here and now and gives me the impetus and strength to use the time I have well. For Levinas death is inaccessible to light and overwhelms me—it marks the demise of "the subject's virility and heroism"[20] I become weak and lose my courage as I face imminent death. Heidegger sees the awareness of death as a source of strength and encouragement. By owning the truth that I cannot avoid or bypass death, I rid myself of the illusion that my life on earth is going to drift on indefinitely. In facing the fact that the nothingness of death awaits me, I learn to cherish the time given to me and I am liberated to live it in a deeper way. Knowing that one day I will no longer be, I give more care and attention to the fact that for now, at least, I exist. For Levinas death extinguishes any possibility on my part. Dying robs me of all possibilities. For Levinas then, death leads to humility.[21] I am passive in the face of death. I face something that does not issue from myself. This something is beyond the sphere of the world, beyond the realm of what I can understand: this something is mystery. In this passivity vis-à-vis death, I lose my mastery and my powers. I even forfeit my very power to have power. Death is not susceptible to assumption or appropriation. The otherness of death cannot be cancelled by virtue of my assimilation of it, for the alterity of death is not a temporary or disposable quality of death. In death I am in relation with that which is absolutely other. Although the future of death lays hold of me, I cannot lay hold of it. Neither can I anticipate such a future or project it. I cannot take pride in the future as my future. This future that death manifests is disconnected with my present, and so death does not give time to me. In fact, by rendering me passive with a passivity that makes me powerless—"we are no longer *able to be able*"[22]—death deprives me of an essential element of my identity as a person.

Levinas shows how overwhelming and extinguishing death can be. But in Christianity death is not the final word. Re-invoking Genesis, we can say that we are not immortal because of anything we have achieved—after all, we are only dust to which God added his vivifying breath—but because God has made us in his image and likeness. As images of God, we are given the gift of sharing in God's immortality. In talking of the soul's immortality, we can also benefit from the theologies I have mentioned above. Remembering Barth and Cullmann, we can endeavour to keep talk of the immortality of the soul faithful to the vision of the Bible; remembering Metz, we can avoid becoming individualistic when discussing immortality of the soul; remembering Gutierrez, we can ensure that immortality of the soul has repercussions in our world of injustice and social inequality and speaks to the suffering of the poor. These three pressing concerns are acknowledged in two contemporary theological approaches to the soul's immortality: those of Karl Rahner and Joseph Ratzinger. But before we turn to Rahner and Ratzinger, let us first turn briefly to the issue of the soul's separation from the body at death as well as casting a glance at some of Thomas Aquinas' insights on the matter.

Can the soul separate from the body at death? It may be hard to imagine. But it is also hard to envisage that the body repeatedly separates from the soul during life, despite the fact that this separation occurs with unfailing regularity. Such an enormous percentage of our cells are renewed each year (e.g. we shed and re-grow our outer skin cells roughly every 27 days, giving us on average of almost 1,000 new skins in our lifetime, an incredible turnover considering that in four square centimetres of skin there are three million cells) that scientists tell us every seven years we have a completely new body. This means that even the oldest body we see, however wrinkled and frail it may be, cannot be more than seven years old. This fact is even more astonishing than the fact that during the time an average person takes to read this sentence, up to 50 million cells in their body have been replaced.

Although the ancient Greeks did not realize that each human being had a new body every seven years, they did know that the body constantly renewed itself over the course of a lifetime. In Plato's *Symposium* for instance, Socrates quotes the priestess Diotima as saying:

> Even while each living thing is said to be alive and to be the same—as a person is said to be the same from childhood till he turns into an old man—even then he never consists of the same things, though he is called the same, but he is always being renewed and in other respects passing away, in his hair and flesh and bones and blood and his entire body.[23]

The Greeks also came up with a dilemma that speaks to the issue of identity in the midst of change, and which has implications for the soul. The ancient Greek historian, Plutarch, recounts the famous Greek legend about the ship of Theseus, the legendary king of Athens. Theseus sailed to Crete, slaying the Minotaur and rescuing a group of Athenian prisoners in the process. In honour of Theseus' exploits, the Athenians preserved the ship and sailed it on parade each year. Over the years they needed to repair it. They took away the old decaying planks and replaced them with new and better timber, installing new sails, replacing

tackle and rigging, and so on. To explore the radical implications of the repair and renovation of the ship, we can con-
duct a thought experiment. Suppose that at a certain point in
time, every material thing in the boat had been replaced so
that it was made up of entirely new material. At that point
was it still Theseus' ship? Or was it a different ship? And if
it was a different ship, at what stage did it cease to be
Theseus' ship?

We tend to regard the ship as the same to the extent that
it is the same functional structure, even if various materials
or all of them have changed. Once it fulfils the same intended purpose, we consider it to be the same ship. We can apply
this belief about the ship in an analogous manner to the
human being. To be a human being is not to be a certain sort
of material, for we know from science that the material we
are made up of changes completely many times over the
course of an average lifetime. Rather to be a human being is
to be a certain structure or configuring order, what the
ancient Greek philosopher Aristotle would have called a
form. Obviously this form is not a thing, but rather the way
we are, the manner in which the material composing us is
organized into a functioning whole. Aristotle did not regard
the matter of a compound substance like a human being as
essential to it, but as merely accidental, a conviction which
harmonizes with the findings of science about the replaceable nature of the human body cells. But he did argue that
the form of a compound substance like a human being was
essential to it, making the person precisely what she or he
is.

Thomas Aquinas, the Italian giant of medieval philosophy and theology, was indebted to Aristotle for his teaching
on the soul, though Aquinas also clarified and developed

points that remained obscure in Aristotle's philosophy. Aquinas' great achievement in his thinking on the soul was to preserve both the fundamental unity of human nature by stressing the intimate union of body and soul,[24] while also allowing for the kind of distinction between body and soul that assured the soul's endurance in the aftermath of physical death. Let me give a quick overview of what Aquinas has to say. Since his scholastic terminology can often present a formidable obstacle to understanding his thought, I will avoid the technical terms he uses as much as possible. Thomas Aquinas accepted the Christian doctrine that each human being has a soul and believed it was unnecessary to provide a philosophical proof for the existence of the soul. He was intent on describing the character of the soul and its relation with the body. Aquinas argued that persons were neither mere souls nor mere bodies. We always meet *ani-ma*te bodies (with the accent on the Latin word for "soul", *anima*) and in*carn*ate souls (with the accent on "flesh" *carne*). The soul and the body are one in a way similar to the impression sealed on a piece of wax is one with the wax.[25] In other words, humans are composite beings, a unity of the soul and body. Without the body, the soul could not function in our world. Nevertheless within the overall unity of the person, body and soul are distinct. Furthermore the soul is superior to the body as is evidenced by spiritual activities such as reflecting, judging and choosing. Despite its superiority, it is in and through the body that the soul chooses, knows and loves. But the superiority of the soul does not extend to arrogance—the soul does not simply use the body as an instrument; we are not ghosts in a machine. Were the soul simply a motor driving the body, the profound unity of the human being would be undermined. The individual is a living organism, a composite of soul and body. It is not just the soul that wills, thinks or feels. In the exercise of freedom, knowledge and love it is the whole person, body and soul, who decides, knows and loves. Thoughts, feelings, and sensation are interwoven with the body. We use the same pronoun "I" in phrases such as "I think", "I feel", "I breathe", "I digest", etc. When my body is sick, I exclaim that *I* am sick. When my throat swallows food, it is also *I* who swallow food. Another person does not simply punch my stomach, they punch *me*. And this act of violence does not simply hurt my body, it hurts *me*.

It is because of the soul that the body exists. The soul communicates its being to the body. But it would be inaccurate to say that the soul is in the body; according to Thomas it is more correct to say that the soul contains the body.[26] The soul, as the constitutive force of the body, is present "in" the entire body and "in" every part of it. It is not as though the life of the soul only penetrates the body partially. If there were areas of the body that remained uninhabited by the soul, these parts of the body would be broken down by virtue of being cut off from the soul, just as a leg, once it is amputated, becomes subject to the disintegrating power of nature. It is the soul which gathers and organizes the body, enabling it to exist and function as a body. We owe to the soul all that makes us distinctively human; it is the principle and foundation of our existence as human beings. The soul, which is a living thing, is precisely what makes the body alive. Without the soul there is no body, only a corpse. Because the soul is what organizes the body to function as it does, it is the *form* of the body, not in the sense of being the outward shape and appearance of the body, but in the sense of being the inner, organizing and animating principle of it.

Death does not destroy the soul. Through God's benevolent will, the soul is kept alive after death. It remains the same when the body passes away, like a football team remains the same even if there is a change in all the players, coaching staff as well as the playing ground. Although the soul survives death, there is no complete human being until the resurrection of the body, when the body is re-united with the soul.[27] In the meantime, there is simply the centre of thought and volition. Therefore, an essential aspect of personal identity is lost temporarily with death.

It is obvious that Thomas Aquinas regards death as loss rather than liberation. The soul loses the body at death, and so the human being is not complete afterwards, but partial and truncated. Yet there are already hints of immortality during a human lifetime in the manner in which the soul can act independently of the body.[28] This is evident in the way human knowledge can go beyond the limits of the spatial and temporal frameworks in which we initially perceive things.[29] For example, each one of us has the notion of "music" and it is not a notion that we can hear or see. Certainly the ear can hear many specific kinds of music. But the intellect can abstract from these different types of music and arrive at the concept of music itself. The ear is tied to what is particular and material, whether it is classical music, jazz, blues, Gregorian chant, country and western, pop, rock, rap, or whatever. But the intellect can grasp the essence of these specific things and form the concept of music. Although we hear many types of music with definite sound patterns, the notion of music itself is something that transcends the limits of space and time. It can be predicated of everything from Mozart to Eminem, from Haydn to hip-hop. We can discuss music in abstraction from trumpets and trombones, from bossa nova or boy bands. In order for us to understand the essence of music, our intellects extract that essence from the particular material music we hear. We conceptualise the nature that all these different types of sounds have in common, a nature which allows them to share in the description "music". When this happens, the sense of hearing no longer plays a role; now it is the mind which grapples with the notion of music. The soul is no longer operating as the form of the body, but is functioning independently and separately. Were our minds purely material, they would be unable to extricate themselves from the specific music they hear. They would only hear particular kinds of music as the human ear does. But because of the soul, this immaterial principle within, we can extract the essences of things that we encounter in the world around us, divest them of their spatio-temporality, and give them a meaning which transcends the boundaries of space and time.

A different kind of argument in favour of immortality advanced by Aquinas centres on the natural indestructibility of the soul. Normally, a compound entity made up of different parts ceases to exist when it disintegrates or dissolves into the elements of which it is comprised: for instance, a dilapidated building gradually crumbles and falls apart. But the soul is simple in nature because it is non-material. This is evident in its operation of thinking, as we have just seen. Although our concepts depend on experience, in other words we understand by virtue of ideas that we abstract from our sensations,[30] it is nonetheless true that in every act of thinking and willing, the soul can act independently of the body. In the introduction to this book we came across a graphic example in Jean-Dominique Bauby, author of *The Diving Bell and the Butterfly*, who suffered from locked-in syndrome, as a result of a fearful stroke that left his body paralysed while his mind remained active. Although he was unable to live a bodily life, Bauby led a rich life of the spirit; locked in physically, he was able to wander freely with his memory and imagination. Other recent examples include Nelson Mandela, whose quarter century in a South African prison showed that physical confinement does not necessarily imply imprisonment of the spirit; and Viktor Frankl, the Jewish doctor who realized that even in the brutality of a Nazi concentration camp, he was still free to choose his attitude and to transcend interiorly his external destiny. People can rob us of everything except our souls. Since the soul is without matter, it is not like a body which is extended in space, which is divisible, and which has a particular shape. The soul is without extension and shape, as well as being indivisible. Because it is simple and not composed of different elements, it cannot be destroyed of itself.

But there are things in the world which are destroyed because of the destruction of another entity upon which they essentially depend. For instance, the beauty of a statue can fade because the stone in which it is chiselled becomes eroded. But this cannot happen to the soul. Because of its spiritual nature, the soul cannot be destroyed through the destruction of the body with which it is united. This is because of the independence of the soul from the body, since despite its unity with the body, the soul is not material and does not intrinsically depend upon the body. Ultimately, despite the simplicity and spirituality of the soul which both point to everlasting life, in practice the actual immortality of the soul derives from God, to whom it owes its existence. Though God has the power to destroy as well as to create, it would be inconceivable for him to deprive a human being of the soul which he has given, since this soul is created to last forever, by virtue of the nature with which God endows it.

Recent theologians have found new ways of addressing the question of the immortality of the soul. Karl Rahner, one of the most important Roman Catholic theologians of the twentieth century, did not develop a specific theology of the soul, since he preferred to view the human being as a unified nature. He was critical of the kind of theology that

> speaks of spirit or of man's immortal soul as though what is meant by this were an element within the totality of man which can be encountered immediately and in itself, and distinguished empirically and in test-tube purity from the rest of him.[31]

However, Rahner did discuss the issue of the soul's immortality. By giving a brief summary of Rahner's overall transcendental and anthropological approach to theology, the contours of his picture of soul will acquire sharper definition. Although Rahner is not inclined to use the term "soul" in unfolding his transcendental anthropology, the various terms he does employ have the advantage of highlighting the soul from different angles and with varying nuances. He is fond of considering the human being as one who questions, who is open to being, who is a subject, a creature of transcendence, and so on. Like his onetime teacher Martin Heidegger,[32] Rahner recognizes that the human being is "thrown" (*geworfen*) into the world, existing as part of it, subject to all sorts of unchosen influences, an object alongside other objects. But the soul nature of the human being is already evident to the extent that the human being knows these limits, can ask questions, can put himself or herself into question. This shows that the human being is more than merely a product of circumstances. By repeatedly becoming questions for ourselves, we are already on a journey that has no end, since the questions never die. By recognizing our own finitude, we break through this very limitedness and already touch infinity by touching our soul. Furthermore when we know something, our knowledge is not simply confined to the object: we are also aware of ourselves as knowers. Even though we rarely articulate this latter knowledge, it implicitly accompanies our individual acts of knowing. Because we can put ourselves into question as well as ask questions and because we are conscious of ourselves as well as knowing, we are structured in such a way that we are open to being. By virtue of this crucial anthropological structure, it is totally inadequate to describe ourselves as determined and unfree. Instead, we are souls in the twofold manner of being persons and subjects, characterized both by self-possession, despite our interrelation with the world, and by the ability to transcend the things to which we are present. In line with Heidegger, who championed the disclosing power of existential attitudes such as anguish, being-toward-death and care, Rahner sees our openness to being and thus our transcendence as particularly manifest in experiences such as guilt, death, loneliness, and love. We are capable of transcendental (in the sense of exceeding immanent reality) experience (in the sense of the self-consciousness of the knowing subject that precedes and accompanies each concrete experience). The fact that we are both self-conscious and surpass immanence points to two important aspects of being creatures endowed with souls.

LIFE AND SOUL

The way in which I have just described Rahner's approach could give the impression of a privatized type of search where the subject gazes inside in order to find transcendence. In fact his approach could be misconstrued as just such a solitary quest because of key elements of his analysis in *Spirit in the World*.[33] But even in this early text, Rahner argues that we are in the world in a spiritually relational manner, either opening ourselves towards God or closing ourselves off from him. Furthermore, he links body and soul into an organic unity by claiming that we are only capable of reaching towards God, that is, we are only spirits, by virtue of being in the world where we live alongside others, speak a common language, and so on. Our experience of God is always mediated through our relationships, through the society, culture and epoch we live in. The very title of the book he published two years later, *Hearer of the Word*, already intimates in a more explicit way that the human being is someone who does not so much look inside to find transcendence, but listens in the hope that he or she will be addressed by God. With the development of his concept of the supernatural existential, the relational dimension of the human being becomes even more accentuated. According to Rahner there is no such creature as a purely natural human being, since the relation with God, whether accepted or rejected, belongs to the essence of being human. Because of the universal salvific will of God, God's self-communication is constantly at work, and every human being is touched by grace.

Let us turn now to what Rahner has to say about the immortality of the soul. Rahner considers human knowledge and awareness of the inescapable nature of death as already a fundamental factor distinguishing human beings

from animals;[34] in other words, we could say that it is a further pointer to the fact that each human being has a soul.
Rahner does not conceive of the soul as becoming more distant from the material world after death, but instead more
integrated with it. This idea is not as revolutionary as it
might first appear, if we consider that already during earthly life the soul is constantly open toward the world, inter-
acting with it, and communicating with it by virtue of being
an enfleshed soul, a soul that is corporeal. During life itself
we already exhibit the dynamism to humanize ourselves by
relating to others. Therefore despite the difficulty in imagining or visualizing a posthumous deepening of the earthly
union between the soul and matter, it has at least a certain
plausibility. Rahner visualizes the soul as becoming all-cosmic after death rather than non-cosmic,[35] realizing a profound bond with the material world. He does not mean by
this that the whole world becomes a "body" for the soul, as
its own body is a body for it during life. Neither does he
mean the omnipresence of the soul in the universe. Rather
he means that the soul, no longer tied down by an individual bodily structure, has a new freedom to relate and to open
itself in a deeper and more comprehensive fashion to the
world.[36] In this sense, Rahner's notion of immortality is not
about escaping from the world, but about relating to it in an
even more intimate manner.

Let me simply articulate one implication of Rahner's
all-cosmic stance, an implication which he himself did not
address, but which speaks to the concerns of liberation theology without abandoning the concerns of the soul. If, as
Rahner suggests, immortality of the soul involves a deeper
relation with matter and history, it also entails a deeper
awareness and concern for the oppression and injustices

that plague our culture. Since death offers us the possibility of definitively entering into the mysterious otherness that is God, we thereby become closer to the heart of the world. Thus rather than removing us from history, death brings us to a greater comprehension, understanding and love for those who people it. Therefore the next life is not so much a refuge for the soul from the tragedy and suffering of earthly existence, but an invitation to care more deeply for an existence that has not been left behind but rather appropriated more deeply as a result of dying. This care is not simply an idle looking on but is active and involved in the spirit of Saint Thérèse of Lisieux's famous promise to spend her heaven doing good on earth. In this sense, Rahner's all-cosmic soul is not immune to the imperative of liberation theologians for action on behalf of justice in the here-and-now. Rather this soul is both spiritually alive and historically engaged, while avoiding the Scylla of disappearing entirely into an unreal and ethereal sphere and the Charybdis of being reduced to purely humanitarian concerns.

Joseph Ratzinger—now Pope Benedict XVI—no doubt conscious of the critiques of figures such as Barth and Cullmann, does not start out by conceiving of the soul as an immortal substance, although the path he takes does lead to the affirmation of the soul's immortality. Ratzinger begins by identifying the particularity of the human soul with the fact that it makes us capable of authentic dialogue with God. It is because of this capacity for divine dialogue that the soul is immortal.

For 'having a spiritual soul' means precisely being willed, known, and loved by God in a special way; it means being a creature called by God to an eternal dialogue and therefore capable for its own part of knowing God and of replying to him. What we call in substantialist language 'having a soul' will be described in a more historical, actual language as 'being God's partner in a dialogue'.[37]

The dialogue of the soul with God is a conversation of love, and true love entails immortality: "All love wants eternity, and God's love not only wants it but effects it and is it."[38] It is through the relationship of the human being with God that he or she escapes self-centredness, and rather than remaining self-encapsulated in anxiety and fear, opens out to God. The very fact that God is a God of the living rather than the dead is already a pointer toward human immortality.[39] The confirmation of human immortality is given by the fact that the human being, by virtue of being a creature that is endowed with the privilege of contemplating and loving God who is immortal, thereby shares in God's immortality. Therefore rather than deriving immortality from a consideration of the soul in itself, Ratzinger endorses the biblical conception, founding immortality in the personal relationship between the human being and God. "Immortality as conceived by the Bible proceeds not from the personal force of what is in itself indestructible but from being drawn into the dialogue with the Creator"[40]

In Ratzinger's view, although the soul leaves the physical body behind after death, in another sense it remains connected with the body understood as the incarnation of the personality that the human being has developed in the course of life. The soul therefore retains a connection to matter, even after death. Ratzinger seems to envisage something akin to an assimilation of the body into the soul after death, by virtue of which the material element is transmuted to a higher level. Borrowing from Teilhard de Chardin's insight into evolution as a personalizing process that culminates in a communion of love, Ratzinger sees the power of love at work in its elevation of biological life or *bios* to life as *zoe*,[41] in other words, to a definitive and spiritual life characterized by love and freedom:

> the essential part of man, the person, remains; that which has ripened in the course of this earthly existence of corporeal spirituality and spiritualized corporeality goes on existing in a different fashion.[42]

According to Ratzinger, because the person is not an isolated soul but only finds selfhood in being with others, the future of the human being after death will only be truly realized when the future of humanity also finds completion. As in the case of Rahner, this conviction of Ratzinger is not at all inimical to the quest for justice in the world and the hope for the ultimate fulfilment of history, when there will be liberation from sin and from sinful consequences that enslave humanity. No person is entitled to be an island of self-concern and indifference to others, even after death. Each person is embedded in human relationships and in a temporal framework. Because these relational and temporal contexts are part of the essence of the human being, neither of them is discarded with death. Although the person who dies thereby leaves the current of history, his or her relationship with history is not abolished. But as well as the culmination of the story of humanity, Ratzinger also envisages a sublime destiny for all of creation. In this regard, he sees the resurrection of the body as an expression of the truth that all matter will not simply be combined in a neutral or external matter with spirit, but will itself as material become spiritually elevated and fulfilled. The history of matter will become subsumed in some yet unforeseen way with the history of spirit, although the exact nature of this fulfilment of matter cannot now be conceived by us.

These theological approaches to the soul's immortality are undoubtedly stimulating and energizing, but in modern society those who believe in an afterlife do not envisage such cosmic scenarios. They tend to see heaven as a confirmation and intensification of earthly joys and comforts. What images of the immortal soul, if any, percolate through to the secular world? In order to answer that question adequately, an exhaustive survey would be necessary. However, in order to give a taste of the kind of images that are prevalent today, let me just advert to a recent bestselling novel which depicts immortality in a secular way. The main character in the novel is a dead girl. And she narrates the story from her vantage point in heaven. *The Lovely Bones* (2002) by Alice Sebold begins thus:

My name was Salmon, like the fish; first name, Susie. I was fourteen when I was murdered on December 6, 1973 . . . It was still back when people believed things like that didn't happen.

The novel subscribes to the belief that the human being is made up of body and soul. Susie is brutally raped and murdered by a bland and monstrous neighbour. As she dies, her soul leaves her body, and as it is ascending to heaven, it brushes the body of her classmate Ruth, who ever afterwards remains fascinated and intrigued by Susie. What about Rahner's talk of a deeper relationship after death between the soul and the world? On the one hand Susie has a more profound connection. Sitting in her gazebo in heaven she can watch all the people she knows on earth. She knows not only their words and actions but can also discern their thoughts, feelings and dreams. On the other hand, Susie is more cut off because although she is deeply aware of what is happening on earth, she herself is simply mourned as a loss by the living. She is frustrated by the fact that those on earth cannot communicate with her and are indeed oblivious to her presence. However, with time she discovers small ways in which to make her presence felt and to communicate indirectly with the various characters. Although Susie initially finds out that the one thing she cannot do in heaven is to rejoin her family and friends back on earth, ironically it turns out after a while that her family and friends never cease sensing her presence.

Susie's soul is immortal since she outlives death. However, God does not guarantee her immortality for the simple reason that there is no divinity of any sort in her heaven. It is assuredly a God-free zone. This heaven reflects a religion-less religion, spirituality free of faith. There is no Saint Peter to welcome her at the gate, no angel to accompany her in. Instead Susie is helped to adjust to her new surroundings by a matter-of-fact intake counsellor called Franny. It is as though therapy has become the opiate of the inhabitants of heaven. In any case this heaven is politically correct, certain not to ruffle members of different faiths, little faith or even none. No souls are judged in this heaven. There is no word on what happens to murderers and killers. Perhaps everyone is eligible. Pet dogs are certainly welcome, and Susie has an emotional reunion scene with her canine companion Holiday when he arrives.

In its own idiosyncratic way, Susie's heaven is like a whimsical take on Jesus' promise that in his Father's house there are many mansions (John 14: 2). This is because there are different heavens in this novel, which seem to be self-enclosed entities. For instance, the daughter of Susie's favourite teacher died a year before of leukaemia, but Susie never meets her, possibly because Susie's heaven is tailor-made just for her. The buildings are exactly like the suburban high schools she likes, there are playing fields with soccer goalposts and female javelin throwers. There is a school with no textbooks save for her favourite magazines—*Seventeen, Glamour,* and *Vogue.* The only class she has to attend is the one she enjoys most: art class. Peppermint stick ice cream is available all the year around. But Susie is not an isolated soul in this personal heaven. She shares a duplex with a girl who plays the saxophone. She has lots of friends. They talk and laugh and tease each other.

In Ratzinger's theology, the individual soul does not find ultimate fulfilment in the absence of a definitive cul-mination to history for the whole community of humankind. Although this reality is not to be found in *The Lovely Bones*, there is nevertheless a faint secular echo of it. Susie's heav-enly future is left hovering until she achieves closure with her earthly life. After her murder, her parents' marriage starts to fall apart, her siblings go through a difficult period, and her killer goes on to murder other innocent girls with impunity. Justice needs to be done and different people and relationships need healing. Therefore, despite the fact that all her other wishes can be realized instantly in heaven, her desire to see accounts settled on earth must wait. She has to watch patiently as events there unfold according to their own unpredictable logic.

There is a preposterous scene late in the novel where Susie's soul comes down from heaven to inhabit the body of her schoolmate Ruth, so that Susie can consummate her relationship with her childhood sweetheart Ray. In the context of the novel it strains credulity that a fourteen year old girl whose final and traumatic earthly experience was a murderous rape might find the prospect of returning to earth for a single act of sexual intercourse so inviting. From a Christian point of view, such a case of bodily possession could only be diabolic in nature. Souls of people in heaven can only appear again on earth by God's express command. Spirits from the lower regions only return through the work of human beings dabbling with occult forces joined to satanic powers. But these latter spirits never bring truth, only falsehood.

The life of Susie undergoes change in heaven, but no transformation. Her heaven reflects her dreams as a 14 year old on earth. There is no qualitative leap, no decisive shift of horizons. She merely enters into a more comfortable and cosy version of what she already knew on earth. What is endearing about Susie's heaven is that it is a good place. Her soul arrives at a good destination. The great English mystic Julian of Norwich believed that all would be well. What is disappointing about the immortal soul of Susie is that it does not go beyond our complacent assumptions regarding reality. It enters into a mediocre comfort zone. The real heaven, however, is pure bliss, so real that our world is practically fake by comparison, so joyful, that our happiness is sadness by contrast, so ablaze with love that our affections are only ice that melts in the face of it.

Susie only yearns for an imperfect good, for a partial beatitude, because it is still an egoistic good, and this is why her heaven looks more like purgatory, and why she must wait until she has definitively let go of people on earth before she can ascend to heaven in all its fullness at the end of the novel. Thomas Aquinas provides an argument for the soul's survival of death that is based on a much stronger desire than the desire evinced by Susie: it is the human desire to achieve perfect happiness and thus everlasting life. This natural desire of the human being cannot be empty, vain or without purpose, according to Aquinas. Obviously this would be a useless desire if it could not be realized; but in fact nature does not lie. This desire presupposes the existence of a reality that corresponds to it or fulfils it. But it is evident that this desire for complete happiness cannot be perfected in this life. The only alternative is that it must be perfectible after this life.

To make this argument for immortality of the soul even more graphic, imagine the following scenario. A mother sits by the hospital bed of her six year old daughter who is dying of leukaemia. She is heartbroken to see her daughter on the threshold of death and finds herself wondering about human mortality and the prospect of an afterlife. Which of the following two alternative possibilities would this mother want to envisage? 1. My daughter is created and formed by God, and destined by him to enjoy another life after this one, a life that will last for ever, so that I can live in the hope of rejoining her after death, if I continue to believe in God and to live in his love. 2. Ultimately my daughter is no different from an animal that is born, mates, and dies. When she breathes her last she will turn into rotting flesh and decompose, as will I. We will no longer be, and shall never see one another again.

It is clear that the mother would want to behold the first possibility. Thomas Aquinas would not regard this first possibility as the blind faith of a desperate mother. Nor would he regard this maternal instinct as the product of an irrational drive; it is not the yearning for some imaginary state that lacks reality. Rather this woman's belief in God and the wonderful new life he promises is built upon a longing that is intelligent since it is rooted in what is most distinctively human about her: it is embedded in her soul. It is not a longing that she accidentally acquired. This mother, like all human beings, has the natural human desire to exist forever. This natural desire explains why even human beings who refuse to believe in an afterlife are nevertheless keen to see their philanthropic deeds or artworks or scientific inventions or good names outlive them. Even though they proclaim disbelief in an afterlife, they nevertheless expend time and energy to ensure an immortality of sorts for themselves. They cannot avoid testifying to this inner and inescapable natural desire that God implants within each of us. It is God who implanted this natural desire for continued life in this woman. Her desire for an endless life of happiness along with her daughter makes sense because it is the longing for something that exists, and it is a yearning that will be fulfilled.

A different type of example could also add weight to Aquinas' argument for the natural desire for immortality. It is a concrete historical example of harrowing human suffering and injustice. The victims of the Holocaust did not receive consolation on earth. Neither did many of their oppressors receive retribution. Although the lives of these victims can become meaningful for survivors and future generations, inspiring them to say "never again" to such inhumanity, their lives can have no meaning for the victims themselves if there is no afterlife that redresses their suffering. As regards their oppressors and murderers, most reasonable people have an innate sense that wrongdoers and criminals who escape justice on earth must be ultimately accountable in the beyond. Therefore, there is an inherent conviction that the perpetrators of these horrible deeds will face an eternal court, even if they elude a human one.

In its own small way, the novel *The Lovely Bones* shows that those whose lives are cut short and destroyed do find healing and closure in another life. Their earthly lives acquire meaning and sense because of eternity. Alice Sebold can dare to give her novel such a hopeful title because despite the fact that Susie's body is brutally dismembered after her death, there is something lovely about how she is knitted together again in eternity and the manner in which the lives of those she loves interlace anew in a healing way.

Ultimately, belief in the soul's immortality is not a way of denying the importance of life on earth. Because our actions on earth are so decisive in shaping our eternal destiny, the limited time at our disposal is of the utmost importance. The fact of immortality endows the mortal journey with unbelievable significance. Life was given to human beings that they might burn with love, and not become tepid with unfulfilled good intentions or lukewarm because of opportunities missed. The ethical message of the immortality of the soul for the here and now is "don't waste life."

4

Beauty and the Soul

"People are moved to wonder by mountain peaks, by vast waves of the sea, by broad waterfalls on rivers, by the all-embracing extent of the ocean, by the revolutions of the stars. But in themselves they are uninterested."

Saint Augustine, *Confessions*[43]

Being an image of God is about much more than being simply an inert copy; it is about being a living replica, so penetrated with God's goodness that the glory of God is naturally radiated to others. For Christians, Christ is the paradigm and exemplar, since he "is the image of the invisible God" (Colossians 1:15). Although God's image is perfectly incarnated in Christ, it still needs to be realized by Christians. Each of Christ's followers (to adopt the "already/not yet" tension used by theologians to describe the kingdom of God) is both *already* an image of God and *not yet* one. The image of God is simultaneously a present reality ("whoever is in Christ is a new creation"—2 Corinthians 5:17) and a future truth (we are all "being transformed into the same image from glory to glory"—2 Corinthians 3:18). It is the image of tomorrow from which Christians are invited to live today. Believers do not visibly see the glory of this image of God inside of them and in others. It is not fully manifest. Although it is invisible for believers, they must act as if they see it, they must believe in it. Most of all they must strive to beautify this image (putting on "the new self, which is being renewed in knowledge in the image of its Creator"—Colossians 3:10), all the while trusting that God will help them.

The soul, a gem of God, is beautiful and good. But beauty does not always imply goodness. Unfortunately, for something that offers such delight and pleasure, beauty of itself is profoundly ambiguous. When we describe somebody as beautiful or handsome, we may hope and believe that their beauty is also indicative of goodness and truth, but in fact we know that by ascribing beauty to that person, we are not necessarily implying a high degree of moral perfection. We often want to believe that everything that is beautiful is also good, which at times makes us susceptible to deception. The truth is that, however eloquently we wax about beauty, however sublime it seems to us, none of this can take away from the fact (although flowery prose and beautiful appearances may successfully camouflage it!) that there may be only the barest connection between beauty and goodness. Certainly beauty can attract people towards goodness, but it can also glorify evil, making vice more attractive than virtue.

This twofold character of beauty is evident in the Christian understanding of Satan. According to Christian tradition, Lucifer's beauty was initially allied with goodness, but no longer is. This angel, whose very name signified "bearer of light", was originally the most beautiful and perfect of God's creatures, but he became proud of his beauty. Although scriptural evidence for the primordial story of Lucifer's fall is tenuous, the lamentation in Ezekiel 28:12-17 is one of several passages often cited. This lamentation personifies the ancient civilization of Tyre (a prosperous and dominant power in the sixth century B.C.) as an arrogant king whose pride shall be humbled. At another level it has been taken to refer to the fallen angel, a reading which has plausibility to the extent that this extract from Ezekiel talks of a created being, an anointed cherub, who was a perfect creation, excelling in wisdom, of astonishing beauty, yet had a violent spirit and was cast out of God's dwelling because his beauty led to pride and his splendour corrupted his wisdom. In stories of temptation from the lives of the saints, Lucifer has been known to appear to them initially as a beautiful being. However, despite his perfect form or appearance, sooner or later he reveals himself as repellent. One of the reasons that his beauty is so seductive is because we can easily confuse beauty with goodness: common to both is perfection of form. But in the case of Satan, his beautiful exterior is not the radiance of truth or goodness but the misleading mask of evil and falsehood.

In the mythological world of Greek antiquity there are already intimations of the ambivalent character of beauty. Its fatal charm is expressed in the famous story of Odysseus and the Sirens in Homer's *Odyssey*. Despite their repulsive physical appearance, these nymphs perched on a rocky crag enchanted sailors with their beautiful voices, luring them to their deaths. Odysseus stopped the ears of his men with wax in order that they would hear nothing, and had himself bound to the mast of his ship with orders to his men not to release him under any circumstances until they had left the Sirens' island far behind them. Odysseus found the music so beguiling that he nodded to his men to untie him from the mast, but they only bound him tighter and kept rowing until they were well out of range of the Sirens' voices. However, beauty does not only seduce mythological characters toward evil. It also can also be used to cast a spell in the real world. For instance, the Third Reich used the beauty of the music of Bach, Beethoven, Brahms, Mozart, and Wagner as propaganda for their skewed politics and inhuman racial ideals.

Obviously physical beauty is not bad in itself, and naturally we all admire it. And generally we do not experience it as masking evil, though it often functions as a distraction from the good. For instance, living in a culture which has not so much exalted the body as set particular versions of the body—the beautiful body, the thin body, the sexual body, and so on—upon a pedestal, our attention can be led away from deeper levels of beauty. Saint Augustine of Hippo's famous lines from the *Confessions* suggest how the beauty of created things can divert our attention from Beauty itself:

Late have I loved you, beauty so old and so new: late have I loved you. And see, you were within me and I was in the external world and sought you there, and in my unlovely state I plunged into those lovely created things which you made. You were with me, and I was not with you. The lovely things kept me far from you, though if they did not have their existence in you, they had no existence at all.[44]

In the context of the ambiguity that is especially attached to physical beauty, it is vital to stress that I am not proposing fervour for beauty alone. Bereft of goodness, beauty has no moral density. It is only in the case of God that beauty and goodness are in perfect harmony; since of his nature God possesses all perfections, he inevitably possesses beauty as well, and to a degree that is mysterious for us, since it is infinite.

In the Gospel of Matthew (Chapter 23: 25-26), Jesus berates the scribes and Pharisees because they wash only the outside of the cup and plate; inside they continue to be consumed by greed and self-indulgence. It is as though the scribes and Pharisees imagine that external hygiene automatically confers inner cleanliness, and so they do not bother about the latter. Today the cult of beauty is prey to a similar confusion and inversion of values. Our culture confuses the body with the spirit, taking the body to be the spiritual centre of the human being, and so it neglects the life of the soul. We are encouraged to take more care of the body than of the spirit—the focus is on externals, not on what surges from inside. Yet it is the spirit that is especially made in the likeness of God, who is spirit. Even to respect the spirit as much as the body would be already a great advance.

The body is more seriously harmed by greed and lust than by a nose that is not perfectly aligned or lips that are not red-blooded and full. But there are voices within our culture and ourselves that entice us to commit all kinds of sins with carefree abandon, and meanwhile to seek plastic surgery in order to remedy minor blemishes. However, it is wrongdoing which truly defiles the body, the temple of the soul, where God intended the Holy Spirit to be enthroned instead of cheap idols.

God invites human beings to do the kinds of good works which reflect the divine breath imparted to our species on the day of creation, because these are works that will live for ever. But the sorts of deeds which remain at the level of the dust from which human beings were made, the clay they have in common with animals, will be dispersed by the winds of time. Although both body and soul are created in the divine likeness, since God created each, it is especially the inside that is marked by its resemblance to God.

The theology of Saint Augustine evinces, more than any other, a deep and abiding awareness of the human being as the image of God, as a reflection of divine beauty. Augustine was especially gripped by the verses from *Genesis* that we explored in Chapter Two. Augustine saw beauty as perfectly present in God, as replicated in the human soul, and as present in a less vivid and real manner in the human body and the rest of creation. Although Augustine saw the Trinitarian image reflected much more in the soul than in the body, he nevertheless was glowing in his admiration for the beauty of the human body. A classic instance of this is to be found near the end of his monumental *The City of God*. Augustine begins by drawing attention to the upright stature of human beings that invites them to focus on things above, as well as to the dexterity of the tongue in speaking, eating, etc., and to the hands in writing, carrying, gesturing, etc., all of which conspires to confirm the excellence of the soul they serve. But apart from highlighting the body as a servant of the soul, he also enthuses about the proportion and symmetry of the body itself, even in its minute and hidden parts, which suggest that God created it more for the sake of beauty and dignity than in the interests of necessity and usefulness.[45]

Not only because of its intimate association with the soul, but also because it is an intrinsic part of a human's nature, the body deserves honour. Augustine says so much in *The City of God* in the context of stressing the importance of honouring the bodies of those who have died. Their souls may have departed their bodies, but their dignity is still intact:

> For if a father's ring, robe, and the like, are the dearer to children the greater their affection for their parents, human bodies, which are more intimate and close to us than anything we can wear, are by no means to be spurned. These are not merely for man's adornment or convenience; they are part of his very nature.[46]

However, God's beauty is reflected in a supreme way in the soul of the human being, which comprises the trinity of memory, understanding and especially will.[47] It is in the combination of these three faculties that we are most faithfully in the image of God. Let us look at each of these faculties in turn. For Augustine, memory has a larger meaning than the one we ascribe to it today. It includes recollection of the past, self-consciousness in the present, anticipation of the future, imagination, emotions, as well as the subterranean world of the subconscious. Augustine marvelled at the breadth and depth of memory, which in turn led him to stupefaction at the vastness that was inside himself:

Great is the power of memory, an awe-inspiring mystery, my God, a power of profound and infinite multiplicity. And this is mind, this is I myself. What then am I, my God? What is my nature? It is characterized by diversity, by life of many forms, utterly immeasurable. See the broad plains and caves and caverns of memory. The varieties there cannot be counted, and are, beyond all reckoning, full of innumerable things.[48]

Augustine's *Confessions* as an autobiographical text is itself a work of memory in all the expansiveness that word has for him, and is punctuated by a grand paean to the mystery of memory in Book Ten. Augustine cannot see an end to this immense power of memory, and it leads him to gasp in astonishment that mortal human beings could have such enormity of life inside of them. In musing about memory, Augustine does not become enclosed in himself. The beauty of memory is that the more of this vast palace we visit, the more we discover that this palace is also inhabited by God. The more Augustine ponders the more he realizes that God is not beyond memory, but in his very soul. Delving into the apparently introspective world of memory enables us to open our lives to an infinite horizon, just as the intensely personal nature of Augustine's *Confessions* makes them so wonderfully universal.

There are two principal kinds of knowledge or understanding for Augustine: the knowledge that comes through the senses and the knowledge that grasps eternal truths. Let us consider sense-knowledge first. The senses are bombarded by numerous impressions over the course of a single day. We would be totally overwhelmed if there were no central inner faculty to coordinate and integrate all these manifold stimuli (Aristotle called this internal synthesizing faculty "common sense," a potentially misleading expression today since it can be confused with sound practical sense). If the integration of such diverse sense-data seems a matter of course, this is because we have forgotten how fragmented they appeared to us as young children and how much more laborious it is at a young age to make the appropriate links.

The first page of James Joyce's semi-autobiographical novel *A Portrait of the Artist as a Young Man* shows how sensory stimuli reach the infant Stephen one by one. He makes connections between these stimuli on account of their proximity to him and to one another, but primarily because of his inner organizing faculty. Although this novel is told from a third-person perspective (except for the final 6 or 7 pages), we nevertheless discover the world as Stephen does and in the manner that he encounters it. The tiny Stephen, called "baby tuckoo" by the family, first *hears* his father tell him a story about a "moocow that was coming down along the road."[49] Then he *sees* his father looking at him, and he notices that his bearded father has a "hairy face". Because he is so young, Stephen is not aware that the moocow is simply an imaginary creature and he presumes that it had come down the road where their neighbour Betty Byrne lived. We are then introduced to *taste*, as we discover that Betty Byrne sold sticks of lemon-flavoured sweets. And finally the sense of *touch* and *smell* are mentioned: "When you wet the bed first it is warm then it gets cold. His mother put on the oilsheet. That had the queer smell."

Despite his tender age, what Augustine would call Stephen's rational soul manages to receive these happenings, though he has not yet combined them into a fully intelligible ensemble. However, Stephen's soul does manage to construct a modicum of coherence and meaning—Aristotle's faculty of common or central sense is already at work in Stephen, an internal sense that synthesizes and configures the innumerable stimuli coming from the external senses of touch, taste, hearing, sight and smell. This can be seen by the manner in which the boy distinguishes between sound and vision, taste and touch and smell. Obviously he cannot distinguish sound from vision with the sense of hearing itself, for the sense of hearing can only perceive sound: Stephen cannot see his father's hairy face by using his own ears! Neither can he distinguish sound from vision via the sense of sight, since Stephen cannot *see* sound. Therefore, he must be able to separate these senses in his mind with the help of another sense which can perceive both. This sense is the internal sense called the central or common sense. But Stephen has something that transcends even this central sense; he has a reflex consciousness which enables him to distinguish himself from the objects around him. Stephen knows that he is the one who sees, touches, hears, and so on. He is aware of himself as a single person experiencing these jumbled events. If the various stimuli seem random and almost capricious, at least there is the stability of identity, the personal "I" that is Stephen, to give continuity and context. Stephen already possesses the ability to understand things in such a way that they make sense to him, and acquire meaning for his mind, even if this involves a certain deviation from the reality of how things really are. For example, Stephen sings for himself the song that is taught to him, making it his own, even if it means that he mispronounces it and changes the lyrics "*O, the wild rose blossoms*" that he hears into the green rose of his own song. It

is a song to which this young child clearly claims owner-
ship: "He sang that song. That was his song. *O, the green
wothe botheth.*" Stephen is even using his memory in the
large meaning that term has for Augustine. Not only does he
remember (inaccurately) the song that is taught to him, but
he simultaneously shows imagination by re-shaping it with
creativity.

According to Augustine, the soul is the faculty that
organizes sense impressions in a meaningful way; the senses themselves do not do the organizing. The eyes themselves are not aware that they are seeing nor are the ears
aware that they are hearing. Augustine argues that sense-
perception implies that we have a soul that acts through the
senses, while being distinct from them.[50] This is what is
happening in the case of the fictional character Stephen.
The sensory events described on the first page of *A Portrait
of the Artist as a Young Man* reveal someone who is sensing
these events. Despite Stephen's baby talk, he is not so much
at the mercy of his senses as already mastering them.

But apart from the knowledge that comes from the senses, Augustine also believes that there is a superior intellect
in the human being, a kind of reason that is an illumination
from God. For instance, it is because God enlightens us as
to what perfect wisdom is that we can judge whether someone is wise, it is because God's light teaches us what beauty is that we can judge something to be beautiful.[51] In the
ninth book of Augustine's *Confessions* there is a marvellous
example of this illumined reason at work in the moving
description he gives of his mystical conversation with his
mother Monica while they are waiting at the port of Ostia
near Rome for a ship to Africa. Monica never boards this
ship for she falls ill five days later, and soon afterwards an

everlasting ship ferries her away. The setting for this mystical experience is the house in which they are staying on the Tiber. Mother and son are gazing out of a window that overlooks a garden. No one else is around. They ascend beyond the first kind of knowledge that is mediated through the senses to go beyond the limits of the senses, "and in a flash of mental energy attained the eternal wisdom which abides beyond all things."[52]

According to Augustine, the beauty of the soul as the image of God is most of all to be found in the will, in desires, and in love. It is difficult to overestimate the importance of the will in the life of the soul, for it is through the will that we make decisive choices, mould our characters, and become who we are. Although Augustine believes in the free will, he is not hopelessly idealistic. He realizes that the will expresses its freedom most of all at the level of desire and intentionality, and not at the level of executing decisions. For example, an alcoholic is free to decide to give up drinking. However, when it comes to the implementation of this decision, other factors intervene—the alcoholic may not want to admit that his life has become unmanageable, he may be reluctant to examine his conscience in an honest way and to admit to himself and others how much he has messed up his own life and harmed theirs, and so on. In a similar way, Augustine recounts in his *Confessions* how he wanted to convert in principle but was hesitant to do so in practice, exemplified by his famous "give me chastity, but not yet" prayer.[53] Augustine's vices personified themselves as voices inside of him, pulling and tugging at his resolve to convert, suggesting to him that he would never be able to live without them. Augustine saw no way to break his old habits until grace inspired him to see that he must not rely on his own will-power and strength, but turn to God for help (just like the steps in Alcoholics Anonymous demand a recognition of one's helplessness and a dependence upon a higher power).

Stephen Dedalus in *A Portrait of the Artist as a Young Man* is a character of strong and insistent desires. The artistic beauty to which Stephen wants to devote himself has strongly libidinous overtones. Wading through the shallow water on the beach at Dollymount Strand in Dublin, the adolescent Stephen sees a beautiful birdlike girl, whom he describes in decidedly sexual terms. It is a moment of revelation for him; here, standing in the salty water of Dublin Bay, he experiences his aesthetic baptism. "Heavenly God! cried Stephen's soul, in an outburst of profane joy."[54] Turning away from the girl and striding across the stand with his cheeks flaming and his body glowing, Stephen feels called to be an artist, to generate and reproduce life. Stephen now regards beauty as his religion and creed, and later declares in coldly proud words that echo those attributed to Lucifer: "I will not serve."[55] Stephen sees himself in grandiose terms, as a priest of the immortal imagination, exercising a similar function to that of the priest over bread and wine: in Stephen's case, transubstantiating perishable matter into art that will never pass away.

Unlike Stephen Dedalus and possibly James Joyce, Saint Augustine does not oppose earthly beauty and God as arch-rivals for our affections. Instead, Augustine recognizes that God is the origin of the beauty of created things and God himself is beautiful. So it is not a matter of rejecting worldly beauty as an evil, but of seeing it in analogical terms, as simply a flickering ember of beauty as compared to the all-consuming fire of God's beauty. This is evident in the following question that Augustine asks God, and in the answer that follows (notice here how Augustine uses the senses: what he sees, hears, smells, tastes, and touches):

> But when I love you, what do I love? It is not phys-
> ical beauty nor temporal glory nor the brightness of
> light dear to earthly eyes, nor the sweet melodies of
> all kinds of songs, nor the gentle odour of flowers
> and ointments and perfumes, nor manna or honey,
> nor limbs welcoming the embrace of the flesh; it is
> not these I love when I love my God. Yet there is a
> light I love, and a food, and a kind of embrace when
> I love my God—a light, voice, odour, food, embrace
> of my inner man, where my soul is floodlit by light
> which space cannot contain, where there is sound
> that time cannot seize, where there is a perfume
> which no breeze disperses, where there is a taste for
> food no amount of eating can lessen, and where
> there is a bond of union that no satiety can part. That
> is what I love when I love my God.[56]

Since God is beauty in all its perfection, the desire for beauty need not be an obstacle to the spiritual journey, as long as we learn to ascend from the beauties of creation to Beauty itself. Augustine's soul was never free of desires and longings. He knew that the beauty of the human soul was not perfect. It did not reflect God as a perfectly calm sea reflects the sun. Instead it was like a surging ocean full of tumultuous waves and obscure depths. But Augustine, crucially, recognized his inability to free himself from his self-centred desires. In confessing his powerlessness Augustine was graced with a deepening and re-channelling of his desires.

The Swiss theologian Hans Urs von Balthasar views the mission of Christ through the prism of divine glory. He believes that if Christ's radiance, beauty, glory, and splendour are stressed, they can inspire a response of reverence and service in the human being. Beauty needs to be included in theology if people want to develop souls that are beautiful in virtue, because without beauty the good becomes devoid of attraction, and no longer seems worthwhile. Indeed it is not only the good that loses its sway, but truth becomes robbed of its force of conviction as well.[57]

But not any kind of beauty will do: the beauty that von Balthasar proposes is divine beauty. This is not something superficial that simply exists in order to induce pleasure or evoke a fleeting response. Instead it is radically subversive: Jesus Christ turns all accepted measures of beauty upside down. This is because the beauty of Christ is visible most of all at what is seemingly the ugliest moment of all: Jesus' tortured death on the cross. The beauty that shines in the form of Christ at that moment is the beauty of infinite love. It is Christ's self-surrender to the Father in identification with sinners. This beauty seeks to touch people and to transform them, to awaken and to draw them. The response it elicits is not sensual and momentary but all-encompassing, one that embraces the individual's entire existence. This beauty is a light that pierces the heart, issuing a moral summons like the one described by the poet Rainer Maria Rilke in the "Archaic Torso of Apollo": "you must change your life." The summons enjoined upon the beholder of this crucified beauty is nothing less than the invitation to re-shape and mould anew an entire life so that it may conform to this new standard of beauty.

Although von Balthasar's emphasis on beauty is not new (as he argues in the second and third volumes of *The Glory of the Lord*, such a theology is present in some of the most creative theologians in Christendom), it is novel for a modern theologian to stress it. But what distinguishes von Balthasar especially from theologians of previous epochs is the importance he explicitly assigns to intersubjectivity, to the "I-Thou" relationship, to being as "being-with" where the hyphen acts analogically to an umbilical cord irrevocably linking the individual to others. Von Balthasar's theology is not peopled with solitary souls. Although this distinguishes him from the theological trend of previous centuries, it unites his perspective with that of the Bible.

I believe we can analogically apply the beauty von Balthasar predicates of Christ to the human soul. Why? Because the human soul shows forth the image and likeness of God. Thus the splendour of the soul remains essentially mysterious despite what we intuit of it. T.S. Eliot's poetic creation J. Alfred Prufrock speaks of "the eyes that will fix you in a formulated phrase." We cannot pin down the soul, it cannot be grasped and encompassed. Our knowledge of it will always be fragmentary and partial because of the infinite profundity and inexhaustible richness of God in whose nature it shares. Indeed we could say that the ability to perceive the soul is a gift of God. And so we cannot grasp it in knowledge, but at most find ourselves being grasped by it in a spirit of reverence and awe. Furthermore, the mystery of the soul increases with increasing revelation. Just as we listen to the music of Bach again and again without ever plumbing its depths, so it is with our soul. However much we find out about it, its essential mystery is inexhaustible, since there is always more to discover. Thus the soul paradoxically shelters its ineffability even in revealing itself to us.

The light of the soul wells up from the inside. Although the soul is like God, it is not God. God is essentially incomprehensible. The soul walks a tenuous tightrope between comprehensibility and mystery. There is an element of comprehensibility emanating from its interiority that nevertheless does not undermine the soul's fundamental incomprehensibility. The soul neither disappears totally into mystery nor is it wrenched away from its essential mystery by reason. The beauty of the soul ultimately resides in the striking harmony between the finiteness of the loving gestures of the person and the infinity of God that these gestures reveal. This beauty is not accessible to the dispassionate spectator or the scientific observer. It presupposes receptivity and the capacity to allow ourselves to be taken up into a dynamic movement, to allow ourselves to be swept into a different plot of meaning.

The beauty of the soul can survive the ugly and tragic dimensions of life. These vicissitudes of life do not necessarily damage the soul. The only thing that wounds the soul and disfigures its beauty is doing evil. Indeed, from a spiritual point of view, the difficulties of life could be viewed as a kind of beauty that is difficult to enjoy and the harmony, proportion and order of which are only intelligible in retrospect. For instance, there is the temporary ugliness of the cross and its ultimate beauty, the temporary tragedy of Jesus' death but its enduring glory. The kind of beauty that embraces suffering is already to be found in the great Greek tragedies of Aeschylus, Sophocles and Euripides. There is always a resolution of contradictions at the end of their tragedies. But this resolution is never a merely theoretical reconciliation. It is profoundly real: the discovery of light in the midst of terrible darkness, the knowledge that the gods command our destinies and thus, however unrelieved our sufferings, we can nevertheless attain serenity because everything that happens somehow reflects the splendour of the divinity. There is beauty because when the protagonists of these tragedies come to realize that their lives are bathed in the light of the gods, they are thereby ennobled.

There are a couple of outstanding examples in Sophocles, often regarded as the most truly classic of the great trinity of Greek dramatists. In *Oedipus at Colonnus*, Sophocles has Oedipus pronounce these "beautiful" lines to King Theseus:

> I come with a gift for you,
> My own shattered body . . . no feast for the eyes,
> But the gains it holds are greater than great
> beauty.[58]

In other words, Oedipus has a beauty to offer that far transcends beauty in the sense of something merely decorative, attractive or aesthetically pleasing. In *Ajax*, Odysseus contemplates the immense suffering and death of Ajax, and it is as though a beautiful fragrance arises from the shattered existence of Ajax, inspiring Odysseus to a love that goes beyond duty: "I will be as much a friend as I was once an enemy."[59] The stark beauty of these Greek tragedies continues to cast a spell over Western literature. In his 1990 version of Sophocles' *Philoctetes*, entitled *The Cure at Troy*, Seamus Heaney adds some verses of his own after line 1484, where he hopes against hope for "something beautiful" in the midst of the troubles in Northern Ireland:

History says, 'Don't hope
On this side of the grave.'
But then, once in a lifetime
The longed-for tidal wave
Of justice can rise up,
And hope and history rhyme.[60]

These Greek tragedies point to theology. In their case
the religious background is both unsurprising and
inescapable since tragedy itself derives from religious ritual. The beauty they evoke is also religious—it is a saving
and transfiguring beauty that is founded upon the Greek
gods. The night of suffering the heroes undergo is only
endurable because it is the night of the gods and thus,
although the night is devoid of the power of seeing, it is also
illuminated with an empowering and a divine presence.

The greatest souls become more beautiful when they
emerge from the crucible of suffering. Like Christ, they fall
like grain into the earth, only to rise as ripened fruit. God's
omnipotence is especially manifest in the fact that he trans-
forms the destructive power of death into a source of life
and blossoming. Because of Christ the dissolving power of
suffering does not lead to dissolution but to a reshaping and
new configuration. The crouching caterpillar acquires the
wings of a butterfly and the beauty of the soul is set free.

5

Beyond the Fortress Soul
and the Fragile Soul

*"They that hope in the Lord will renew their
strength; they will soar with eagles' wings; they
will run, and not grow weary, walk, and not grow
faint."*

(Isaiah 40:31)

Some contemporary intellectuals dismiss the soul outright
as a religious myth or reduce it to a biologically conditioned
process in the central nervous system. Many others,
although they do not talk specifically of the soul, in effect
use related terms such as the ego, the self, the subject, subjectivity, the free agent, consciousness, self-consciousness,
spirit, and so on. These terms, although sometimes used as
synonyms of one another, have different nuances of meaning. Indeed any one of these terms taken in its own right can
have a plurality of meanings, depending on the presupposi-
tions and perspectives of the different thinkers that utilize it.
These terms, then, neither harmonize necessarily with one

another nor do they always display an inner consistency of meaning.

It comes as no surprise that none of these terms coincides with the Christian understanding of the soul. However, many of them overlap with the Christian conception in significant and decisive ways. As in the case of the soul, many of these terms imply intelligence, freedom, a broadly spiritual dimension to humanity, and at times even an immortality of sorts. In this chapter when I talk about the challenge of moving beyond the fortress soul and the fragile soul, I am using the word soul in a way that overlaps with such various terms as subject, ego, self, and so on, without thereby reducing the superabundant meaning of the word soul to any one of these terms. Not only is the word soul rich in meaning; it also possesses a productive ambiguity, by which I mean that it has deep reverberations, implying mystery, evoking depth, and all the while remaining elusive, so that it ultimately escapes definition. By being productively ambiguous, the word soul both evokes these other terms that describe what is distinctive about the human being as well as retaining an enigmatic substratum.

At the beginning of his profound study of the nature of personal identity, *Oneself as Another*, the French thinker Paul Ricoeur (1913-2005) contrasts the exalted subject with the shattered or humiliated subject.[61] Ricoeur describes how Descartes placed the subject upon a pedestal, making it the foundation of all knowledge and the source of all certainty, so that it became a kind of mini-god. He then argues that Nietzsche exaggerated in the opposite direction, totally undermining the subject to the extent of humiliation. I believe that Ricoeur has identified two important currents in thinking about the self: the modern era inaugurated by

Descartes which was triumphal in its vision of the self, and the postmodern era which has deconstructed and destabilized the self out of all recognition. When I talk of the modern era, I am thinking of an era in which the self is self-certain, secure in its possession of the truth, confident that it can control the world, trusting exaggeratedly in rationality, monolithic in its mentality, suspicious of any diversity that threatens an overriding uniformity, and so on. By the postmodern era, I mean an epoch in which the self has become decentred and deracinated, where its perspectives have moved from fixity to fluidity, where it no longer trusts the large frameworks of meaning provided by nation, religion, rationality, history, and so on, but instead privileges small-scale and multiple points of view such as local or individually shaped criteria of value.

Inspired by Ricoeur's comparison, in this chapter I want to reflect on the flawed nature of the fortress soul, a notion which is still pervasive in our Western culture. I will then look at how one recent thinker, Emmanuel Levinas, has tried to go beyond this by ushering in a fragile soul. Although Levinas does not want to destroy the self as Nietzsche's hermeneutics of suspicion did, he comes perilously close to doing so. This will bring me to argue that the way beyond the pitfalls posed by both the fortress soul and the fragile soul is to adopt the loving soul.

I use the phrase "fortress soul" in the hope that this metaphor may graphically express a sensibility that is pervasive in modern culture to the extent of shaping our self-understanding. The image of a fortress is a shorthand way of expressing a sensibility that is evoked by words related to fortress such as solidity, certainty, protection, consolidation, elevation, isolation, exclusion, fear of others, anxiety, aggression, hostility, and so on. Descartes, often called the father of modern philosophy, is one of the principal sources of this way of considering ourselves. Descartes found unshakeable metaphysical certainty in the ego, subject or soul, a thinking thing or *res cogitans*. The fortress soul is a *subjectum*, having the connotation of the substratum or invariable condition which grounds everything else. It denotes power and mastery. Everything is transparent to it, and it is self-transparent. Everything else is an object for it. In its more extreme forms, the fortress soul is not only the ground of everything and the source of knowledge, but is also independent of the ties of history. There is always the risk that this fortress soul will be no more than solitary and solipsistic, cut off from fellow human beings, from history and from the world. The fortress soul carries connotations of mastery, control and deletion of what is other and different. The ego, at least, before Freud, tended to be viewed as "master in its own house."[62] It is likely to be viewed as an origin. It needs to be associated with a dimension that is beyond knowledge and appropriation. It tends to be viewed as cognitive, thereby excluding other aspects of the human being—emotion, desire, the body, etc. The fortress soul needs to open itself up to these other dimensions. It needs to be shaped by the encounter with what surpasses it, namely the meeting with other human beings, and most of all God. The fortress soul, although acting upon the world, also needs to recognize that it undergoes transformation through the world.

Traditional philosophy often works under the presupposition that the self is unified, sufficient, and essentially unproblematic. As in Descartes, the problems are to be found in the hostile world that threatens the fortress soul.

The Romantic movement that swept across Europe in the eighteenth and nineteenth centuries is a good example. Jean-Jacques Rousseau famously declared in the first sentence of *The Social Contract* that "man is born free, and he is everywhere in chains." According to Rousseau, societies enchained the person morally, economically and politically. They alienated the person from the original freedom of the state of nature. Rousseau argued that civilization had corrupted human beings, compromising both human freedom and individuality. William Wordsworth's poems glamorized the stance of the solitary individual whose aloneness heightened his or her prospects of salvation. Romanticism exalted the individual at the expense of society, and stressed self-reliance, emphasizing the innate goodness of the human being. But a fortress can also be a prison, a kind of existence that is endured rather than chosen. And the gift of liberation needs to come from beyond the self. An essential dimension of the self is to be transcendent, to surpass its actuality. In a culture where the fortress soul reigns, even the demands of morality are subordinated to the quest for individual consolidation and personal fulfilment, and our lives are deprived of depth.

Paradoxically, the apparent strength of the fortress soul conceals an overriding weakness. Turning back to Descartes for a moment, it is astonishing (and generally overlooked) that his drive for certainty was fuelled by the threat of an all-encompassing doubt and reinforced by the malign spirit he conjured up in his imagination, a malicious demon who was trying to deceive him totally. Descartes' way to establish certain knowledge was by doubting everything, and this doubt has left its mark on the fortress soul. Descartes proceeded by three stages. First, he noted that the evidence of the senses might be mistaken, as for example when we presume a straight stick is crooked because it is in water. This means that it is possible to doubt the knowledge that comes to us from the senses. Secondly, he remarked that there are no definite traits to distinguish dreams from waking experience. Therefore my belief that I am sitting down writing a book could be a pure figment of my imagination, since I might in fact be asleep in bed. This means that the physical things I take to be real may not exist at all and furthermore the external world itself may not be real. Thirdly, he imagined an omnipotent and evil demon completely intent on deceiving me. If such a malicious spirit successfully deceived me, this means that anything and everything I believed in would be untrue. Each successive stage in these three levels of doubt is more comprehensive than the previous one. Descartes raised the stakes each time, because he wanted to doubt in such a radical manner that whatever he came to believe in the face of such extreme doubt would truly be something indubitable.

The one certainty Descartes is left with in the face of these intensifying levels of doubt is the assertion *cogito, ergo sum* ("I think, therefore I am"). Even if everything I think is false, it is nonetheless true that I think. It is impossible for me to doubt without thinking. And if I think, then I also exist. The *cogito, ergo sum* also neatly answers the ever starker challenges posed by the three successive stages of doubting. The assertion "I think, therefore I am" does not depend on the evidence of the senses, so it is immune to that first level of doubt. But "I think, therefore I am" is also invulnerable to the second stage of doubt, because it does not depend on the existence of an external world. And this truth is also unassailable by the third level of doubt, for if a malign demon deceived me about everything, such a spirit could not deceive me about the fact that I existed; for in order to be deceived, I would have to exist in the first place.

Descartes did not doubt for the sake of doubting or in order to wallow in doubt. Rather he doubted in order to arrive at a sure starting point. Possibly for this reason, and because of the power and renown of his method, we remember Descartes' steps of doubt as just that, steps on the way to certainty. We look back on his hypothesis of the malign spirit as a temporary thought experiment. And yet these doubts and this ghost continue to haunt the fortress soul. The fear behind Descartes' certainty has not disappeared. Descartes' soul may have promised one sure fortress in an unsure world, yet despite this bedrock of certainty a sense of nebulous uncertainty has endured. The fragility at the heart of Descartes' fortress has not gone away. The fortress, although seemingly invincible, is terrifyingly precarious, facing the constant threat of being undermined. In other words, the fortress soul, not only in its origins, but also in its further development, is also a fragile soul.

It is because this fallibility exists that there is a radical questioning of the fortress soul taking place in contemporary culture. Modern thinkers sense fragility, even capitulation, in the formerly secure fortress soul. In his anti-autobiographical autobiography from 1975, Roland Barthes (1915-1980) asked "himself" the following arresting question: "Do I not know that, *in the field of the subject, there is no referent?*"[63] Barthes suggests that the subject is purely linguistic; if it exists beyond language, this existence cannot be articulated. Michel Foucault (1926-1984) wagers that the self will be washed away like a face of sand on the seashore.[64] Cognizant of the difficulties of defending subjectivity, Ciaran Benson,

119

in his recent work *The Cultural Psychology of Self: Place, Morality and Art in Human Worlds,*[65] situates the self in the imaginative world of art, narrative, morality and emotions. For all that, contemporary thinkers do not reject the subject out of hand. In the words of the controversial French deconstructionist Jacques Derrida (1930-2004):

> To deconstruct the subject does not mean to deny its existence. There are subjects . . . This is an incontrovertible fact. To acknowledge this does not mean, however, that the subject is what it *says* it is.[66]

But long before philosophers started asking probing questions, novelists already sensed the deep-rooted vulnerability of the fortress soul. Those who best posed these questions were the writers who had emerged from the cocoon of the fortress soul. The great nineteenth century Russian novelist Fyodor Mikhailovich Dostoevsky was imprisoned as a young man and condemned to death by firing squad. On 22 December 1849, at the age of 28, Dostoevsky was marched to the Semyonovsky Square in St. Petersburg along with his companions, where the sentence of death was read out. A sword was broken over their heads, and having put on the white shirts of execution, they were tied to posts and blindfolded. Seconds before they were to be shot, a messenger arrived with a last-minute reprieve from the Tsar. Little did Dostoevsky and his fellow prisoners know that this mock execution in front of a staged firing squad had been planned from the beginning. The sentence was commuted to several years' hard labour in a Siberian camp.

Dostoevsky's near-death experience and his years of penal servitude in Siberia helped to make him a novelist of genius, enabling him to go beyond glibness and complacency and to face the bewildering and labyrinthine life of the human soul.

In 1862 Dostoevsky visited the International Exhibition in London. This World Fair had become a regular feature from the middle of the nineteenth century, offering merchants and traders the chance to showcase their products. In 1862 the calculating machine was the major new invention on show. While in London, Dostoevsky visited the Crystal Palace, an enormous construction of iron and glass that had been built to showcase the industrial supremacy of Britain for the Great Exhibition of 1851. The Crystal Palace had been hailed as the dawn of a new era of reason; for Dostoevsky it represented the corrupting power of the new age of industry and science. The awesome impact of this building led people to believe that society was progressing toward perfection. Yet despite this gargantuan sign of social advance, concrete individuals continued to be weighed down by the burden of existence. As though to confirm Dostoevsky's pessimistic view, the Palace was plagued by problems, eventually culminating in the devastating fire of November 1936, in which it burned down.

The contemporary Jewish thinker Emmanuel Levinas was aware, like Dostoevsky, of the crippling weight of existence. Having lost much of his family and millions of his fellow Jews in the extermination camps of the Second World War, he was inescapably aware of the suffering and evil of the world. In the aftermath of such systematic and overwhelming evil, Levinas decided not to conceive of human beings as autonomous and self-sufficient beings.

Thus he developed a conception of the person different from the fortress-like model. Levinas is a postmodern thinker with whom Christian theologians have especially enjoyed conversing and dialoguing. This is because he continually dares to subvert Greek-inspired philosophy with Jewish wisdom, to thrust the passionate otherness of the prophets into the serene sameness of Western philosophy, to question Athens from the perspective of Jerusalem as it were. Indeed Levinas fits uneasily into the postmodern camp. This is because he is less playful that many postmodern thinkers: he recognizes the deadly earnestness of living in the wake of catastrophes such as the Holocaust. He is more committed than many postmodern thinkers because he is constantly seeking the other, and insistently redefining the self in terms of responsibility. Yet despite the biblical inspiration of his ethics, his common ground with postmodern thinkers is evident in his attempt to keep his ethics independent of religious faith, as well as his removal of the self from its easy identification with knowledge and know-how, with presence and power.

Levinas finds inspiration in the goodness of the Hebrew Scriptures as well as in the truth of Greek philosophy. As we saw in the first two chapters of this book, the conception of the human being that clearly emerges from Genesis is a relational one. God himself declared that it was not good for the man to be alone, and created woman. And what distinguished man and woman from the rest of creation was their ability to have a living relationship with God. From a biblical perspective, being created in the image and likeness of God suggests a function more than a nature: the function of representing God's interests, of being custodians of his creation, of responding to God's command and of being responsible.

This relational and functional aspect of the soul finds a strong echo in Levinas' thinking. Levinas' conception of the self differs significantly from the usual conception, since Levinas does not seek to pinpoint or identify a human essence or substance. For Levinas, the meaning of the self is not to be sought in interior life or consciousness. According to him, there is not some hidden self inside of me, a kind of spiritual substance independent of matter. On the contrary: I am only "me" to the extent that I am outside of myself. I am a relational event: I am a response to the other. Indeed I am a response that is a substitution for the other. I am a self-emptying in order to welcome the other. This self-emptying mercilessly exposes me to the wound of transcendence by a surrender that is "more, and differently, passive than receptivity, passion, and finitude."[67] For Levinas, this emptying is a kind of humility that devours me: "It is the consummation of a holocaust. 'I am ashes and dust,' says Abraham, interceding for Sodom. 'What are we?' says Moses, still more humbly."[68] In Levinas' attempt at a non-egological philosophy, the self is no longer characterized by a consciousness which seizes an object, but by a "woundedness" and weakness which opens it up to the other. Levinas' philosophy calls into question the self as cogito, as active and dynamic, and as metaphysical foundation. The fortress soul tends to be the subject of proud initiative; Levinas wants to dethrone the human being from this exalted position. He even speaks of the unravelling of the "proud" ego as the advent of the self.[69]

Levinas gives central importance to the notion of responsibility: each of us is our brother's keeper, even though Cain claimed that the care of his brother Abel had no claim upon him. Levinas disagrees with Cain's stance: this is why he places the self in the accusative. Before the will can exercise itself, the ego is accused. This accusation "strips the ego of its pride and of the dominating imperialism characteristic of it".[70] The other appears before me as an appeal to me to go beyond self-concern, self-pity, isolation and self-indulgence. The other offers me an unexpected freedom: not the freedom to continue to defend my fortress, but the freedom to serve, the freedom to enter into my soul for the first time by responding to the neediness in front of me. Certainly I can choose not to respond to the widow, orphan or exile. They have no physical, economic, political or social power that could force me to intervene on their behalf. The only power these marginalized people have is the power to activate my response of service. Their power is purely ethical: "thou shalt not kill." They reveal my present freedom to be one of self-preoccupation and self-enhancement. If I choose to respond to their plight, I give my freedom a totally new dimension. No longer is it merely a freedom to preserve myself, to advance my own interests, to assert myself over against others; rather now my freedom is truly consecrated because it is the freedom to do good. Thanks to the other, I move outside of my fortress self.

The other shakes me out of my complacency, and in this sense is a divine messenger, "and from the depths of defenceless eyes rises firm and absolute in its nudity and destitution."[71] Even though the other is not divine, it is nonetheless the case that my encounter with the other is the privileged place in which I catch a glimpse of God's trace. In Levinas' thinking, God himself is so far beyond any horizon which I can control that I can never access him directly. The only way to draw near to God is to come close to those who, like God, are most outside of the contexts of life that I can make sense of. It turns out that such persons are above all the widow, the orphan, the stranger, and all those who like them do not fit into neat and tidy categories. Paradoxically, God is only present in my relationship with my neighbour by virtue of being absent from it. God is absent in the sense that I can never tame his mystery by pinning him down with my ideas and concepts. God is present in the sense that the sublime otherness of my neighbour indicates something of the utter nobility and otherness of God. Like God, the other is not a "something" that I can grasp or comprehend, but absolutely other, inaccessible to knowledge. The other is completely mysterious: I can never know the other because the other is essentially unknowable.

Because Levinas sees the self as relational, there cannot be a soul without an inherent relationship toward the other. In discussing Ratzinger's conception of the immortal soul in Chapter 3, we saw how central the dialogical nature of the human being was for him: "The distinguishing mark of man, seen from above, is his being addressed by God, the fact that he is God's partner in dialogue, the being called by God."[72] Since Levinas prefers to speak of God only indirectly through speaking of the other, he highlights the fact that I am called by the other, though not into a relation of dialogue, but into an asymmetric relationship, where I am obliged to respond to the other, irrespective of his or her stance toward me. For Levinas, to be a human being is not to be distinguished by the possession of rationality but by the ability to be for the other, though it is thanks to Levinas' capacity for reason that he can arrive at this insight and articulate it! In this context he stresses that the other is in me to such an extent that I am not myself without the other, and yet this other remains other and is not myself. Levinas wants to end the priority and privilege of the self or the same. In order to express this new awakening, Levinas outlines how the other constitutes me through elaborating the idea of the other in the same. It seems difficult to speak meaningfully of the other in the same. After all, according to Levinas, the other is characterized by its radical alterity, its very otherness. How then can the other be in the same, in such a way that it nonetheless remains absolutely other? Can the other be in the same without some kind of relationship or even confrontation between each term? Since Levinas rejects psychoanalytic theories, he obviously does not regard the other analogously to the Lacanian conception of the unconscious as other, as another subject. Furthermore, given that the other is in the same, am I then characterized by a kind of internal fracture? Although these questions are not adequately answered by Levinas, his idea of the other in the same is nevertheless a daring and imaginative way of attempting to be faithful to the biblical understanding of the human being as inextricably bound up with the lives and destinies of others, while remaining irreducible to them.

Levinas regards the other as being in the same in a manner that is not a question of my possession of the other, as though I could contain or envelop the other in my consciousness. The appropriating mode of consciousness does not describe the way in which the other is in the same. Perhaps with Martin Buber's thought in mind, Levinas also stresses that the other in the same that characterizes subjectivity is not a matter of the reassuring or congenial presence of the other that results from edifying interpersonal dialogue. The other in the same does not bring me serenity or calm;

the other in the same agitates me and ruffles my calm—it is "the restlessness of the same disturbed by the Other."[73] Levinas does assert a kind of internal division in the same because of the "presence" of the other. My identity is disrupted so that I am caught up in the restlessness of no longer coinciding with myself. Selfhood then is *"the other in the same . . .* the putting into question of all affirmation for-oneself."[74] This self-turbulence takes the form of extreme responsibility. In the unimaginable passivity of this relation I am so much for the other that I no longer seek to maintain and preserve my own existence.

Comparing Levinas' model to the fortress soul, we can see that because of the encounter with the other, the soul in Levinas is invited not to live for itself and its own interests. The fortress soul, through seeking to achieve its goals, ends up concurring with itself: its aims result in the recovery of itself, self-affirmation, and self-reinforcement. However, the fragile soul of Levinas is not reinforced in its certainties but expelled from them. The self becomes "homeless," deprived of the security of dwelling, radically dislocated, losing its centre of stability, forced into a space that is no longer its own. This exposure to the other, where I am unreservedly offered without any possibility of protecting myself, is vulnerability. It is older than any beginning I can inaugurate and precedes any present. Therefore it cannot be reduced to my initiative. This vulnerability is a reversal of self-certain identity; now I no longer discover protection in any fixed state or consistency; instead I am uprooted from myself and can no longer rest in myself. In an allusion to the suffering servant of Isaiah, Levinas asserts that "the one is exposed to the other as a skin is exposed to what wounds it, as a cheek is offered to the smiter."[75] This exposure is much more than skin-deep. It is so extreme that Levinas describes it as the splitting of a nucleus into parts.[76] I no longer have a nature or interiority, of which I have been deprived. Rather my soul is evoked by a series of qualities that attain hyperbole: vulnerability, defencelessness, unimaginable passivity, an ever more exposed exposure, and so on.

But Levinas' fragile soul goes too far. I become so responsible for the other that I have always another response to give, I even have to answer for the other's responsibility. To be an ego is not to posit one's identity in the nominative form but rather to find oneself in the accusative, constantly implicated and unable to evade one's responsibility. I find myself accused before I can speak in my own name.[77] I become so "non-indifferent" to the other as to be obsessed[78] by the other. The wound of obsession festers inside of me and consciousness cannot get rid of this "thorn in the flesh of reason, the shudder of subjectivity."[79] Proximity reaches its apogee when my restlessness forgets all reciprocity in my relation to the other, like someone in love who does not expect any return. At this peak of proximity it is no longer possible to define the ego; all one can do is to use the word "I," that is, speak in the first person. Although Levinas wants to guard the integrity of the soul in this relation, it seems virtually impossible: because the soul is possessed by an endless desire to be ever closer, it therefore progressively loses any definite and definable shape.

The exposure that Levinas is talking about demands candour; it is the perilous revelation of oneself, "the breaking up of inwardness and the abandon of all shelter, exposure to traumas, vulnerability."[80] The openness it entails is not an openness of information; consequently, it is not the contents of what one says that are decisive. What is crucial is *how* one says what one says. However, it seems to me that this kind of exposure is excessive unless it brings the rewards of recognition and esteem. After all, what people fundamentally ask of each other is acceptance of themselves. They want to know that they are worthy of being cherished. Without a certain minimum sense of being loved or held as worthwhile, they may be afraid to risk growth. Certainly, in order to gain this acceptance, some exposure is necessary, and indeed the reaction to this exposure is unknown at the outset. Nevertheless, the person has the right to expect a sympathetic response, even though there is always the risk of being let down. Without a fundamental sense of self-acceptance, it is hard to believe that we could expose ourselves in such a vulnerable manner. However, Levinas seems to posit extraordinary and exaggerated resources in subjectivity. According to him, even if we approach human beings as objects in the midst of other objects, they nevertheless contain possibilities that exceed the order of being:

> Such conceptual possibilities are *substitution of one for another, the immemorable past that has not crossed the present, the positing of the self as a deposing of the ego, less than nothing as uniqueness, difference with respect to the other as non-indifference.*[81]

In Levinas' view, these possibilities express a disinterest that is beyond essence. Therefore these possibilities cannot be reduced to conditioning or vested interests. Indeed, he claims that these possibilities are recognized by those human beings who can discern, despite the anonymity of society, an identity in their fellow human beings, and who find themselves uniquely and irreplaceably responsible for them. Levinas asserts that this responsibility which nobody else can assume on my behalf makes me in fact the most unconditioned being in the world, since "the ultimate security a foundation would offer is absent."[82] There is no abstract category to which I can appeal as a way of shirking this relentless responsibility. Whatever the models or paradigms proposed by psychoanalysis, sociology or politics, this inescapable core of holiness in the human being remains inviolable. This implies that the absoluteness of the self is not to be sought in unrestricted liberty. Rather, my absoluteness and holiness reside in the fact that I can humble myself for the sake of the other: my self "is sacred in its alterity with respect to which, in an unexceptionable responsibility, I posit myself deposed of my sovereignty."[83] But the implication of Levinas' argument is also that my absoluteness and holiness reside in the fact that I can expose myself to personal disaster through self-abjection in the face of the other!

It does not make sense that a person should risk so much exposure without at least a limited hope that this wager may carry some reward. If the person does not receive some sign that self-exposure will lead to support and recognition, the encounter with other people simply becomes an excruciating apprenticeship in suffering. Thus subjectivity is not only stretched but twisted out of all recognition, to the extent of annihilation. If that is what self-emptying entails, then there may be little left in the wake of face-to-face relationships except a deep and merciless wound. Yet Levinas' conception of subjectivity promotes this uncritical willingness to become the object of such destructive cruelty and barbarism.

The giving of myself is all the more costly because the suffering it entails does not necessarily have meaning. It could be suffering for nothing. The cost therefore is both in terms of personal suffering and in terms of the disturbing possibility of meaninglessness. Levinas believes that this precarious condition bordering on madness is necessary, if I am not to try to regain a hold of myself and once again return to my old nature. This absolution of my identity amounts to a reversal of my endeavour to be "for myself" into an endeavour to be "for the other." This reversal "has the form of a corporeal life devoted to expression and giving."[84] Levinas, however, seems to dismiss too easily the natural revulsion in the face of suffering, conveyed so powerfully by the lines of Dylan Thomas: "Do not go gentle into that good night. / Rage, rage against the dying of the light."[85] There is wisdom in this instinctive will-to-life. Indeed the very fact that I question suffering is not a bad thing; it can be an effort to ascend towards goodness by judging suffering as something that falls terribly short of the good.

For Levinas, the self often seems more humiliated than humble: it utterly abandons itself, it suffers maternally on behalf of the other, and undergoes opprobrium in a passive manner. Apart from the possibility that this self-emptying could be the expression of masochism or of some other psychological disorder, it could also be exploited by others for disingenuous ends. I could end up accepting my own complete powerlessness as well as the unbridled power of the other as the habitual pattern of intersubjective relationships. Indeed the height that Levinas attributes to the other could encourage the self to internalize the sensation of its own inferiority to such a degree that it cooperates actively in the process of its own subordination.

For Levinas, the self is so supple and pliant that it is like the constant loss of oneself that maternity can give rise to. "Maternity is the complete being 'for the other' which characterizes it."[86] Indeed, the self's responsibility for the other becomes a maternity, where the self suffers in the excessive manner of a mother who gives her life-blood for her child. The folly of this motherly care goes to extraordinary lengths: "Maternity, which is bearing par excellence, bears even responsibility for the persecuting by the persecutor."[87] This corporeal subject of flesh and blood is therefore a relational subject. Hence identity is not a matter of confirming the subject in and for itself. Instead identity occurs through being for the other, through "a deposing of oneself, a deposing which is the incarnation of the subject."[88]

Levinas develops a conception of the subject that allows space for the fragile soul, but which also ushers in a humiliated soul. This humiliation is evident in the following statement where Levinas inventively re-appropriates the Latin word *sub-jectum*: "The self is a *sub-jectum*; it is under the weight of the universe, responsible for everything."[89] The self is acted upon to such a degree that it becomes barely recognizable. Not only does Levinas reject the notion of a static or inflexible self that would be an unchanging substratum of experience; he also crushes the human being with the weight of a massive responsibility that it never chose. I am a limited being and yet I contain a call that infinitely surpasses me. Faced with such an infinite obligation, it is hard to conceive how I could surpass my actuality into a dynamic potentiality, and become transcendent, unless we explicitly introduce God and grace into the equation. But although Levinas dances on the frontiers of theology, he does not want to cross the threshold.

Levinas' fragile soul remains within the parameters of the conception he is attacking. This is because he compensates for the excess of appropriation and acquisition in the fortress soul with an excess of passivity. Ultimately, the fragile soul of Levinas, although holy and admirable, becomes too brittle in the face of the severity of the obligation and responsibility which threatens to crack it. Is there a way beyond the fortress soul and the fragile soul? I believe so. It unfurls through a love for one's neighbour that combines features of the fortress soul (e.g. energy, strength, passion, power) with traits of the fragile soul (e.g. vulnerability, risk, self-exposure), without thereby collapsing into either extreme.

6

The Loving Soul

"It is the greatest good for a man to discuss virtue every day."

Socrates in Plato's *Apology*, 38a.

What does it mean to be good? This question is not solely the property and preoccupation of religiously minded people. Nick Hornby's novel *How to be Good* (Penguin: London, 2001) is designed to make its readers ask precisely this question of themselves. In its inconsistent, flawed yet genuine way, the novel asks (without quite knowing how much it is asking or what to name it) whether goodness means transformation instead of change, and whether transformation is even a remotely viable proposition in a liberal middle-class London family at the dawn of the new millennium. Nick Hornby sets himself an ambitious project. Even Dostoevsky found the task of depicting the saintly Prince Myshkin in *The Idiot* a thoroughly daunting and well-nigh impossible task.

The novel opens with a dramatic conversation by mobile phone between Katie Carr, a GP in north London, and her husband David, a columnist for the local newspaper. Katie has been having an affair while at a medical conference at Leeds, and because she considers herself a fundamentally decent and good person, especially given the fact that she has put up with her ranting husband for so long, she reckons that she has a right to at least a minor bout of infidelity.

David is a sarcastic, albeit witty character, a journalist who makes his money writing a regular newspaper column entitled "The Angriest Man in Holloway". And he makes sure to live up to that title. Katie, only intending to remind David to scribble a note for their daughter's teacher, ends up blurting out, to her enormous surprise, that she wants a divorce. In fact Katie and David do not get divorced. A different transition occupies most of the novel. David undergoes a sudden conversion experience at the hands of a flaky New Age faith healer-cum-hippie called DJ Good News, making him a changed man overnight. He lives more simply, reaches out to help the poor, but also displays the kind of smugness that makes you cringe. David's new-found virtue forces Katie to ask herself repeatedly whether she is good at all and what being good means. Katie, from whose point of view the novel is told, wants to be a good person—like most of us. But Katie does not really want to change in the process—again like most of us. In other words, Katie does not want the Resurrection. The Resurrection is not merely about improving the quality of life, it is not simply about making things better. The Resurrection is truly radical. It is a quantum leap and a paradigm shift: it is about transformation.

After his conversion, David decides to refrain from judging others, though unknown to himself he becomes highly judgmental of his wife, family and the middle class ethos to which they have formerly unthinkingly subscribed. Katie finds post-conversion David to be fanatically zealous as he indulges his new hobby of "redeeming souls". He gives away her cash to a homeless child, donates his child's computer to a homeless shelter, and devises a neighbourhood scheme to house the homeless. As for Katie, she espouses sound principles: she believes in being caring toward others, in feeding the poor, helping the homeless, but when it comes to the crunch she prefers to have as little direct contact with them as possible. Katie instinctively knows that her lifestyle is radically out of kilter with her liberal beliefs. But she also is not sure how to move from change to transformation.

Katie's desires are too small and petty. The loving person is someone with generous and vast desires, big enough to reach out towards the infinite mystery that is God. Katie's latent generosity is impeded by a series of valid but limited desires: security and material possessions figure largely. There is a limit to her openness—certain experiences are beyond her ken and she wants them to remain that way. Author Nick Hornby reflects his protagonist Katie in the sense that his thinking on how to be good ultimately suffers from a lack of energy, a fear of risk, a failure of desire. The novel begins with a grandiose and fiery project, but the author finds it increasingly difficult to keep his epic ambitions aglow and fades into a bleak moral twilight. Having shown the limits of various ways of being good, such as the New Age, liberalism, the Church of England, and social activism, Hornby suggests that it is more prudent, even if regrettable, to keep our desires modest and circumscribed. He intimates that the best we can do is to take care of our domestic world; the larger-scale issues are simply too tortuous to negotiate. The novel ends on a pessimistic note. David finds that his enthusiasm for his new way of life has left him. The final words of the novel belong to Katie: "but just at the wrong moment I catch a glimpse of the night sky behind David, and I can see that there's nothing out there at all."

The sky is dark and empty at the end of Nick Hornby's *How to be Good*. According to the Canadian theologian Bernard Lonergan, in order for our sky to become bright and for our horizon to be transformed, we need to be invaded by the gift of God's love flowing into our hearts. When God's love lays hold of us, we become new selves, seeing the world from an entirely new perspective: there is not simply change, but transformation. This affective conversion makes love the foundation and principle of life, so much so that the person becomes ever more fully a being-in-love. Lonergan describes this religious or affective conversion as follows:

> It is an other-worldly falling in love. It is total and permanent self-surrender without conditions, qualifications, reservations. But it is such surrender, not as an act, but as a dynamic state that is prior to and principle of subsequent acts.[90]

This description provides a model and goal for the loving soul. The dynamism of affective conversion guides it toward perfection. It is absolute self-donation with no trace of self-interest, it is complete self-surrender with nothing of the self held back.

I have briefly invoked the theology of Bernard Lonergan. What about the New Testament itself? What light can it shed on the loving soul? The Greek term *agape* is a good place to start. Despite the richness of the English language, we are often content to use a single overarching term—love—to designate realities that can be radically divergent: erotic love, the love of friendship, familial affection, and divine love. Even though the New Testament was written in vulgar or "common" (*koine*) Greek, it was more precise. One term recurs again and again when the discussion is about specifically Christian love, namely *agape*. This term seems to have been more or less peculiar to Christians and, to a lesser extent, Jews. Apparently it was hardly used at that time outside of Judaeo-Christian circles.

Interestingly, the word *eros*, generally denoting passionate, romantic, desiring or sexual love, which was the most common word by far in Greek culture for love, never appears in the New Testament. *Storge*, denoting family love, a kind of tender and nurturing affection, does not appear in the New Testament either, though a variant, *astorgos*, meaning "without natural affection", appears in Romans 1:31 and 2 Timothy 3:3. *Philia*, the term for the love of friendship, is used at times, for example to describe the nature of Jesus' love for the beloved disciple (John 20:2) and for his friend Lazarus (John 11:3). However, it is telling that the first Christians studiously avoided a term (*eros*) that the surrounding culture favoured, while making a point of using a word (*agape*) that was scarcely ever heard among other Greek speakers.

It is not surprising that the first Christians used this special word *agape*, since they were evoking a kind of love that no one could have dreamt of: the utterly inconceivable love, the love born of God. What distinguishes *agape*-love most of all is that it originates with God, for God loved us first (1 John 4:19). No human could have imagined that God would lower himself to become one of us in the figure of Jesus. He is the anointed one who goes out to sinners, the Saviour who reaches out to the lost, the healthy one who turns to the sick. However, he does not become a sinner or lost or sick himself in the process. Rather he comes into our world in order to redeem it, liberate it, and bring it back to God. In other words, Jesus does not enter the world in order to be simply reduced to our dimensions, but in order to enlarge our horizons to infinity. Although innocent, Jesus bears the weight of our guilt, going to the extreme of dying on the cross for our sake.

The pre-Pauline hymn of Philippians 2:6-11 vividly expresses the kenosis or self-emptying of Christ. The pre-existing eternal Son does not cling to the life, glory and power he receives from the Father, but empties himself. The total and loving self-surrender of Jesus on the cross bears definitive witness to his self-giving love. What we witness at that decisive moment of crucifixion is God's power to love to the utter extremity of love in and through the powerlessness of the Crucified Son. Jesus' death of love on the cross is the ultimate act of generosity. Certainly, human love entails actions of extraordinary generosity and self-sacrifice, yet they pale into an almost invisible shadow against the fire of this divine love.

The journey of the loving soul must follow in the footsteps of Christ; it needs to be the definitive movement away from egoism to the utter other-worldly love which is being-for-others. The cross of Jesus is the standard for the loving soul. As Jürgen Moltmann says, "In Christianity the cross is the test of everything which deserves to be called Christian."[91] Jesus empties himself so much that he is total self-surrender, pure being-for-the-other. From a human point of view, this love is beyond understanding, a stumbling block for both Greeks and Jews.

To claim that "God is *agape*" (1 John 4:8) is a powerful claim. To assert that God is *agape* is to say that in his innermost nature, in his very essence, in his way of expressing himself, God is love of the highest and most noble kind. The love which is so limited in human beings is perfect in God. This love becomes more meaningful and receives context and content when we consider that God is not an isolated person living in solitude, but already a unity and community of three persons whose relationship is characterized by *agape*-love. Personhood in the Trinity is distinguished by a form of self-donation which is being-for-the-other. The Father generates the Son ("you are my son, this day I have begotten you," Hebrews 1:5) before all time in *agape*-love, giving himself fully away so that Christ is equal to the Father as the refulgence and radiance of his glory, the very imprint and expression of his being (Hebrews 1:3), the Word or Logos who is God (John 1:1). The Father is self-surrender in the sense that the Son is the Father as given away: "all that you have is mine" (John 17:10). Beholding the Son, the Father loves himself in Christ.

Were this the human love of *eros*, to love oneself in another would obviously be a self-seeking love. However, because it is *agape*-love, it is without a trace of egoism. In fact, by totally losing himself and fully giving himself away in self-emptying love for the Son, the Father finds himself in the Son. The Son receives everything that he is from the Father, and is himself the perfect expression of the Father's endless self-surrendering love. The sole desire of the Son is to return love for love, to offer himself completely to the Father, to give all that he has received from the Father—all that he is—back to the Father. Because the Son is the one who loves the Father from whom he comes and who has given him everything, Jesus describes himself as the one who remains in the Father's *agape*-love (John 15:10).

This *agape*-love is so unimaginably powerful that it makes the Father and the Son into one (John 10:30), though they nevertheless maintain their distinctive identities. This love between both is nothing as tepid as a desire for each other's well-being or even an inclination towards oneness. It is so mysteriously immense that their common love is a third person. In other words, the Spirit personifies the mutual self-surrendering love between the Father and the Son. The Spirit is also the infinite and superabundant expression of the truth that this common self-donation of Father and Son is an inexhaustible source of life.

The loving soul lives from *agape*-love which originates in God, and so is swept along by the infinitely loving current of Trinitarian love. Admittedly the disciple's participation in the life of the triune God is imperfect and partial. Yet the Father does recognize himself in the Christian, since when he looks at his adopted sons and daughters, he also sees Jesus. The Son unceasingly thanks the Father in and through his sisters and brothers. This is because the gift or grace of the Holy Spirit has been poured into the believer's heart (Romans 5:5), producing in the soul a resemblance to God which far transcends the likeness it has by virtue of being created. The believer is re-shaped into a temple of the Holy Spirit and receives the gift of God, becoming a fountain of love that wells up to everlasting life. Saint Paul describes it as putting off the old self and putting on the new.

The life of the soul is this free gift of God's love, called sanctifying grace in the Christian tradition, the grace that makes human beings adopted children of God, inspiring them to do good, and safeguarding them from the death of sin, which is the only death to be feared. This Trinitarian life does not destroy the person but confirms him or her. Selfhood is attained through the appropriation of one's God-relationship, through love. God gives this gift of his love so that the person may develop this gift into the perfection of holiness. The fountain of living water that issues from God becomes an increasingly more powerful current through the good deeds of the person, and pours back into the infinite ocean of God's love. That is why persons can only find themselves and freedom through finding God. The soul has a greater hunger for love than the body has for food and air. As Jesus says: "my food is to do the will of him who sent me" (John 4:34). The soul is not made for something less than infinity, for something smaller than the vastness of love. The soul is so sublime that even the most wonderful fantasy or thought is nothing compared to it. The fantasy and the thought both come to an end. Although the soul has a beginning, it is without end. To be human is to be immortal.

The soul, however, is free. One can become a good person or an evil one. It is because of free will that either choice is open to the person. Good thoughts and inspirations illuminate the noble origin of the soul; evil thoughts and temptations cast darkness. The person who does not live in love becomes a slave, since that person denies who he or she is: the image and likeness of God. This slavery receives concrete form in the unhappiness that pride, envy, greed, gluttony, lust, anger, and sloth bring; in the suffering that a guilty conscience causes; in the anxiety that the driven pursuit for wealth, status, and self-advancement entails. But those who live in love rise above the narrowness of a self-enclosed existence; they re-locate the focus of their lives; their hearts fills out toward infinite dimensions as they realize the image and likeness of God within.

Becoming a loving soul is a challenge: it means taking up one's cross and following Jesus. Suffering is inescapable since Jesus suffered for humanity, leaving an example so that Christians might follow in his footsteps (1 Peter 2:21). Suffering is not necessarily a question of major personal catastrophes. God is like an expert tailor who cuts the cloth to fit the person. For example, at the beginning of Francis of Assisi's conversion, he unexpectedly found himself face to face with a leper. Francis had always abhorred this disease so much that he could not even bear to look at someone disfigured by it. He was filled with loathing as he contemplated this wretched man, covered in putrid sores, his flesh almost eaten away. The overpowering odour that came from this corpse-like figure almost made Francis run away immediately. But he also felt a new sensation inside, an indefinable impulse to go against all his instincts, to give alms to this man and even to kiss him. Francis ended up placing his lips upon the hand of this leper. He put his mouth against the sores of someone afflicted with a chronically infectious disease, without the least fear. This is a symbol of *agape*-love: it is a fearless love, willing to suffer, never afraid of becoming corrupted by what is corruptible, and intuitively sensing that such contact will bring it closer to God. This is the love of a soul that is both a fortress and a fragile entity.

While the fragility belongs to the person, it is God who is the fortress (Psalm 18:2; 91:2). Like the fortress soul, the loving soul is characterized by strength, courage, and determination. This strength is unassailable because its origin is human and divine. Like the fragile soul, it exposes itself to risk and vulnerability. However, this risk and vulnerability are always meaningful: they raise Christians above self-centredness and unite them with Christ.

What is especially interesting and revelatory about this defining episode in Francis of Assisi's life is that the body of the leper disgusted him; yet Francis touched that body with his own body. Although I have entitled this chapter the loving soul, I am not referring to a disembodied soul. It bears repeating that body and soul work in unity, that the soul needs the body to express itself. Without the body, the soul cannot function, since of itself the soul is incomplete and partial. And it is not as though the soul simply uses the body as an instrument. It is the whole Francis who performs this affectionate gesture toward the leper. In fact, the soul is present in the lips of Francis that touch the leper's hand, for the soul is everywhere in the body, not merely in the head or in the symbolic heart.

Suffering is inevitable on the path toward goodness because *agape*-love does not come easily. Sharing possessions and distributing kind words and deeds is one thing, but giving oneself demands much more. Giving oneself entails for-giving and the number of times one is to forgive ("seventy times seven" in Matthew 18:22) suggests that this practice must be unlimited and boundless in nature. Forgiving means that the offended person wants to do good to the person who has hurt them, and also wants to bring them back into the community from which they have excluded themselves through their offence. *Agape*-love is not simply about helping people but about becoming their servant, in a form of service that imitates Jesus by extending to the sacrifice of one's life. *Agape*-love is not only about celebrating the good in others but demands the patient endurance of their weaknesses and mistakes. *Agape*-love is not merely behaving toward others as one would wish them to behave towards oneself, but calls for love towards one's enemies.

These exacting demands of *agape*-love cannot be argued away. Even sceptically-minded biblical scholars believe that sayings such as "love your enemies" (Matthew 5:44) are the most genuine and authentic expressions of Jesus' teaching. This is because such sayings are found in more than one Gospel (e.g. the phrase about loving one's enemies is also in Luke); they are provocative, going against the grain of Jewish teaching of the period as well as of the practice that early Christians would have preferred; they are eminently memorable and so most likely to have been easily recalled when the Gospels came to be written; and they dovetail with the overall import of Jesus' message.

Love is demanding, but it does not impose the level and intensity of suffering that an outside observer might imagine. There is not the oppressive weight that characterizes the fragile soul of Levinas. This is because through loving the person does not feel humanly crushed but divinely liberated. The Gospel is good news because its acceptance and appropriation by the believer bring happiness, the help of God, and the light of a virtuous life to illuminate the way forward. Those who are without hatred experience a sweet lightness of being. Eyes that only see with love and look for love keep the soul pure; hands that stretch out in love are never heavy; lips that only speak words of love help others to fly. Unlike Levinas' responsibility for the other, which must be characterized by complete disinterest, the Christian duty of love admits of reward, even though the payment is not to be sought now but to be hoped for in the next life (Luke 14:14).

Although the New Testament presents us with the ideal of *agape*-love, this love is neither divorced nor cut off from other forms of love such as *eros* and *philia*. In fact, because the human being is a composite of body and soul, *agape*-love is always mixed with *eros*-love. *Eros* is inevitably associated with erotic love, but this term has a deeper and wider meaning. The appropriation of this more expansive meaning of *eros* can enrich the life of the loving soul. With this goal in mind, I now turn to Plato's vision of *eros*. While Plato did not conceive of God as love and indeed was vague about the nature of God, he nevertheless provided an understanding of love that can enlighten the path of the loving soul today. This understanding does justice both to the fortress-like and fragile poles of the soul; it does not reconcile them into a larger synthesis but maintains them in a creative and dynamic tension.

My focus is the myth of the birth of *eros* that Socrates recounts in Plato's *Symposium*. This Platonic myth of the origin of eros is one of many myths used by Plato in his philosophical writings. Three of Plato's most famous myths focus specifically upon the soul: that of the progress of the soul in the myth of the cave (*Republic* 514-515), the eschatological myth of Er (at the end of the *Republic*), and that of the winged chariot (*Phaedrus* 246), which symbolises the form of the soul. Plato is fond of weaving myths into his philosophical discourse because he does not consider myths as childish fictions or mere illustrations, but as stories that tell us of our spiritual origin and destiny. They evoke truths that are on the frontiers of thought, verities that cannot receive adequate conceptual expression. But most importantly, myths touch the soul, helping it to remember things buried deep down inside.[92] They strike a chord at a level deeper than the discursive knowledge of the intellect.

In the *Symposium*, a masterpiece of Plato's middle period and the most celebrated discussion of love in literature, a company of dinner guests makes speeches about *eros* at a drinking party in honour of the tragic poet Agathon, who has just won a contest in drama. After Agathon's flowery but insubstantial speech, it is the turn of Socrates to address the gathering. Socrates explains that he has learned the art of love from Diotima, a mysterious woman from Mantinea, who helped the Athenians to defer a plague for ten years. This is a most telling remark, precisely because it goes against the whole Socratic view of how truth is acquired. It is almost invariably the case for Socrates that the person is already in possession of the truth, and therefore all teachers are simply midwives, helping the individual to give birth to what are in fact his or her own ideas. But this is not the case with Diotima.

While it is true that Diotima's questions evoke answers Socrates already has inside, she also imparts information and knowledge to Socrates that he did not previously possess. For instance, Diotima explains to Socrates the nature and function of mediating spirits (*Symposium* 202d-203a), she tells Socrates who the father and mother of *eros* were through the story of the conception and birth of *eros*, also describing for Socrates in the process the essential character traits of *eros* (*Symposium* 203b-f), and so on. It is evident then that Socrates himself did not understand the nature and purpose of love until Diotima explained it to him. Therefore Socrates has not learned about love through recollection; love is not something the knowledge of which he naturally possesses and the memory of which he can trigger through an introspective process. It is something he receives as a gift from outside of himself, from the priestess Diotima.[93] We have therefore moved beyond a secular humanism (love is possible for human beings through their own efforts) to a clearly religious perspective (human beings cannot achieve love themselves but receive it as a gratuitous gift).

Diotima teaches Socrates that love is not itself a god, since unlike the gods who are beautiful and happy because they possess beautiful and good things, love does not possess such things, but desires them. Love is a mediating spirit, a *daimon*, between immortals and mortals, the gods and human beings. Love belongs to a spiritual world that is situated between the human and divine world. Since he shares something substantial with both, being an inferior god and a superhuman, the *daimon* of love is connected with both in a manner that gives him sufficient influence to draw the gods and human beings together. Love has a priestly role in the sense of providing a link between the divine and the human. For example, Diotima teaches Socrates that these daimons ìare messengers who shuttle back and forth between the two, conveying prayer and sacrifice from men to gods, while to men they bring commands from the gods and gifts in return for sacrifices.î[94]

In order to explain the intermediary nature of love and to outline its essential traits, Socrates recounts the myth that he heard from Diotima about the birth of love. This myth is helpful in the context of our discussion of the loving soul because it keeps this discourse rooted in reality. We have just looked at *agape*-love which is a perfect kind of love that finds its origin in God. However, we live in an imperfect world and we are imperfect selves. The myth of the birth of *Eros* captures our essential poverty, while simultaneously refusing to relinquish our desire for fullness. This myth is about birth, a moment of great weakness, when a new being enters into the world in all its vulnerability. Yet birth is also a moment of tremendous potential.

As this story begins, we learn that the gods are holding a party to celebrate the birth of Aphrodite, the goddess of love, beauty and fertility, a goddess who will not become known for either chastity or fidelity, but will certainly be remembered for her beauty and her revelry. *Poros* (meaning "resource") is in attendance. *Poros* is gifted, superabounding in intelligence and overflowing with ideas. He is also brimming over with nectar and becomes inebriated. To sleep off his intoxication he wanders into the garden of Zeus and falls asleep. *Penia* (meaning "poverty"), who has not been invited to the celebration, has all this time been at the gate begging. She is waiting at the door, penniless, with nothing except her patience. In order to relieve her poverty, she comes up with the plan of lying next to *Poros* so that she may get a child from him. She knows it would be futile to wake *Poros* up, for he would reject her. So, taking advantage of his drunken and somnolent state, she lies down next to him in the garden and conceives *Eros*. *Poros*, the father of Eros, has everything—intelligence, imagination, social grace, self-sufficiency. He is even physically sated after eating and drinking at the feast. The mother of *Eros* has nothing, just the hope of finding some kind of fruitfulness in her life. *Eros*, then, is conceived by the union of two people who have nothing in common and who are worlds apart. The only element uniting them is the accidental fact that both *Poros* and *Penia* arrive at the same place on the same night on account of the birth of Aphrodite, though for radically different reasons: the former to celebrate, the latter to supplicate.

> This is why Love was born to follow Aphrodite and serve her: because he was conceived on the day of her birth. And that's why he is also by nature a lover of beauty, because Aphrodite herself is especially beautiful.[95]

It is because of this fortuitous link with Aphrodite that *eros*-love is inextricably bound up with beauty. *Eros* will always be desirous of beauty, something he does not possess. But because his conception coincided with Aphrodite's radiant birth, beauty will always be the goal of his striving. He will be a disciple of Aphrodite who is the secure possessor of beauty.

Fundamentally the destiny of *Eros* is already marked out by the character traits of his mother and father. Because his mother is always such a vital part of *Eros*, he is characterized by a fundamental poverty. Just as she begged outside of the gate, *Eros* too remains an outsider, a fragile soul.

> In the first place, he is always poor, and he's far from being delicate and beautiful (as ordinary people think he is); instead he is tough and shrivelled and shoeless and homeless, always lying on the dirt without a bed, sleeping at people's doorsteps and in

roadsides under the sky, having his mother's nature, always living with Need.[96]

The loving soul becomes shaped by this kind of poverty and need as well, because Jesus was. Although Jesus did not grow up in abject poverty but in relatively poor circumstances, he nevertheless was born in poverty and lived the difficult life of a refugee and an exile in Egypt at a very young age. During his ministry he lived simply, without a permanent address, outside the safety net of domesticity. To the enthusiastic man who declares confidently to Jesus that he will follow the Master wherever he goes, Jesus replies, "Foxes have holes and birds of the air have nests, but the Son of Man has nowhere to lay his head" (Matthew 8:20, Luke 9:58: the exact same Greek words are found in both Gospels, as though to strengthen the authenticity and import of this declaration). Like the description of *Eros*, Jesus could be easily described as an unconventional figure, practising table fellowship with tax collectors and sinners, entering into repeated conflict with the religious authorities, crucified as a criminal and an outsider, beyond the city walls.

However, *Eros* is also shaped by his father, not so much in terms of his affectivity, where a mother's influence usually reigns supreme, but as regards his particular form of intelligence and resourcefulness. There is something of the fortress soul in the strength he acquires from *Poros*.

But on his father's side he is a schemer after the beautiful and the good; he is brave, impetuous, and intense, an awesome hunter, always weaving snares, resourceful in his pursuit of intelligence, a lover of wisdom through all his life, a genius with enchant-ments, potions, and clever pleadings.[97]

This aspect of the character of *Eros* is not an example for the loving soul in every respect! But there is something admirable in his commitment, which does not waver like water, but can nevertheless adapt itself to differing circum-stances; in his single-mindedness which avoids fanaticism; in his vigorous and ingenious pursuit of goodness and beau-ty. The person who loves has the courage never to give up the hunt, but to keep loving wisdom all through life.

In summarizing the character of *Eros*, Diotima describes him in the following way:

He is by nature neither immortal nor mortal. But now he springs to life when he gets his way; now he dies—all in the very same day. Because he is his father's son, however, he keeps coming back to life, but then anything he finds his way to always slips away, and for this reason Love is never completely without resources, nor is he ever rich.[98]

The two opposites that constitute love are never resolved into a harmonious synthesis. They always exist uneasily and uncomfortably alongside one another. Diotima's resolution is not a solution. It is a tenuous and tense togetherness of opposing tendencies. I find this a help-ful way to integrate the loving soul within the total person. Because the soul and body form a unity that cannot be exis-tentially and practically broken down into simpler elements during the course of human existence, although we can the-oretically and conceptually distinguish between them, love will always be pure because of grace, yet impure because of the human component. We can never separate the soul from the body through a spiritual process of surgical extraction in the vain hope of living in disembodied and undiluted holiness. In fact, taking away the body from the soul would not be an addition to our humanity, but a subtraction from it. The problems that *Eros* experiences because of his double origin never go away: only his father is divine, whereas his mother is human. It is not possible to make antagonistic tendencies into happy bedfellows. The task of becoming truly human demands continual effort and incessant vigilance. It is not an automatic achievement.

This myth of *Eros* is particularly valuable for our discussion of the soul. First of all, it provides a speedy, intuitive and general grasp of the opposites of love: plenty and poverty, as well as of the essential fact that *eros* is a vital and living relationship with beauty and goodness—in other words, love always seeks to go beyond itself to what is good and beautiful. Secondly, it helps us to get in touch with something that is deeper and richer than reason, affecting our lives at a more profound level. It is not that Plato casts reason aside; rather he realizes that reason and rationality cannot offer an exhaustive account of reality. This is because reality also includes mystery, which is essentially irreducible to explanation. By using this myth of the birth of *Eros*, Plato effectively declares that reason must be ecumenical, opening itself to a dimension that is beyond itself. And this dimension turns out to be religious in nature: Socrates' enlightenment is a gift that comes through Diotima, who in her priestly role symbolizes the mediating nature of love. Thirdly, a myth like this can give an enabling structure and pattern to our lives, as the original Greek word *mythos* suggests. It can give us a new plot of meaning to inhabit, a novel way of making sense of our lives. For instance, just because we cannot easily negotiate between our strengths and fragilities, we are not compelled to become apocalyptic in response. We can be generous enough to give space to the inevitable tensions of life and to live discerningly rather than judgmentally with them. The tensions of life are not to be immediately condemned. Concealed, more or less obviously, within these tensions are always germs of hope, hints of our deepest aspirations, and signs of our vitality. The life and longing that characterized *Eros* were propelled by the very contradictions that never ceased to haunt him. Difficulties can only be eradicated from life at the price of losing our humanity.

The culmination of Diotima's teaching to Socrates brings us back to the theme of beauty and the soul that we discussed in Chapter Five. Without rehearsing all the details of the ascent towards the Beautiful itself as described by Diotima, let me focus on a couple of pertinent details. Diotima points out that everyone is pregnant, both bodily and spiritually, and once they attain a certain age they want to give birth (206c). Because love yearns for immortality, human beings want to reproduce, so that through their off-spring they will live forever. According to Diotima, people who are bodily pregnant guarantee their immortality through begetting children. Those who are pregnant in their souls with wisdom, justice, moderation and the various virtues, also desire to conceive and to give birth to what they have inside, through their spiritual children.

Diotima divines an ascending process in the growth of the virtuous soul. As a youth, the loving person should begin by loving a single beautiful body and helping it to beget ideas that are beautiful. Then he should progress to being a lover of all bodies that are beautiful (210b). Next he should come to realise that the beauty of souls is of greater value than bodily beauty, and therefore he should devote his energies to giving birth to the kind of ideas that will make the young better human beings (210b-c). Finally, he should direct his attention to the great expanse of the beauty of knowledge, which will enable him to give birth to wise ideas and truths. This apprenticeship will give him the maturity and robustness to turn his gaze toward beauty itself (210c-e). If we sustain the fidelity of devoting our lives to beholding Beauty itself we will be able to beget virtue in its most authentic sense.

> "Or haven't you remembered," she said, "that in life alone, when he looks at Beauty in the only way that Beauty can be seen—only then will it become possible for him to give birth not to images of virtue (because he's in touch with no images), but to true virtue (because he is in touch with the true Beauty). The love of the gods belongs to anyone who has given birth to true virtue and nourished it, and if any human being could become immortal, it would be he."[99]

Socrates has hardly finished recounting the teaching he received from Diotima when Alicibiades makes his drunken and noisy entrance into the gathering. Despite his inebriated state, Alicibiades' speech is a true *tour de force*. He compares Socrates to the statue of Silenus, which despite its unprepossessing appearance, contains miniature statues of the gods inside. He declares that the melody of Socrates' discourses is divine, enchanting his hearers. He describes how his heart leaps and tears stream down his face when Socrates begins to speak. He confesses how listening to Socrates compels him to admit that his personal failures are what should concern him most. Alicibiades can neither live with Socrates nor without him . . . The panegyric goes on and on, so that it becomes increasingly evident that perhaps Diotima is only a mystifying fiction to camouflage the truth that Socrates himself is the *daimon*, and that this invented character called Diotima was in fact merely one of those innumerable statues of the gods that Socrates conceals inside and plays so closely to his chest.

Socrates gives us the highest humanistic model of *eros*, a model that is tinged with an unclear but deeply-felt religious impulse. He is the lover of wisdom who knows his own ignorance, the one yearning for beauty who confesses his ugliness. He has a foot firmly planted in the divine and human worlds. He is a bridge between both. Socrates can teach us that while remaining human we can simultaneously be divinised by *eros*. This love is a yearning for something we do not possess, a restless aliveness that takes us incessantly beyond ourselves and directs us toward the source of all beauty, which may be God for Plato although he does not explicitly declare as much. However, he does suggest that the contemplation of absolute beauty (which is also bound up with ultimate goodness) will transfigure our lives.

7

The Utopian Soul

> *"A map of the world that does not include Utopia
> is not worth even glancing at, for it leaves out the
> country at which Humanity is always landing. And
> when Humanity lands there, it looks out, and, see-
> ing a better country, sets sail. Progress is the real-
> ization of Utopias."*
>
> Oscar Wilde, "The Soul of Man Under Socialism"

Is the topic of the soul utopian in a negative manner, i.e. talk
about nowhere (*outopia*)? Or is it positively utopian, i.e.
announcing somewhere good (*eutopia*)? There are those
who would discount talk of the soul as utterly excessive, a
useless hyperbole in the twenty-first century, redundant
speculation about something that exists nowhere (*outopia*).
But behind this dismissal are often concealed suspect and
fearful motives or plain disillusionment: people refuse to
countenance a future that might challenge the status quo;
they do not want to awaken possibilities that they have
repressed because of the demanding sacrifices entailed;
they prefer to remain with the inhumanity they know rather

than risk realizing a new kind of humanism that may elude their grasp; they dismiss the very idea of goodness as nonsensical; they have witnessed the collapse of the much-vaunted utopia of Marxism in the final years of the last century, they have doubts about other "-isms" such as consumerism or capitalism, and do not want to invest in another utopia that may turn out to be at least ambiguous or at most barbarian in nature.

It is my belief that we need to discuss the soul because it offers us a paradigm or model to aim after. I am convinced that the soul is a good place (*eutopia*), a space we need to become more familiar with so that we can inhabit it or let it inhabit us in a more conscious and intentional manner. The soul is not utopia in the sense of nowhere (*outopia*), precisely because it has always been present, in myths, dreams, religion, art, music, literature, and as a perpetual question that haunts human beings. The Bible begins with utopia, the Garden of Eden in Genesis. It was the dwelling of Adam and Eve, both created with a soul which bestowed upon them God's image and likeness, and gave them a perfection of grace which was not soiled by the least admixture of disgrace. God gave them an infinite gift which did not make them infinite, since the creature cannot contain the Creator. But their souls, although of minuscule proportions compared to the grandeur of God, were nevertheless perfect in themselves. The first couple was unified in a transparent relationship. Adam and Eve did not experience fatigue, pain, suffering or even death. They were in harmony with the animal world and were surrounded by a luxuriant and fruit-bearing plant world. There were no laws except for one, that of not eating the fruit of a particular tree; there were no institutions because there was no need for them.

This utopia was destroyed when the first human beings went against their creaturely status and tried to equal God through disobeying the only command God had set. After the fall of the first couple, utopia was transformed into its opposite, *dystopia*. Although souls are still created as perfect and complete by God, they are born with a hereditary stain because of their descent from the first couple. The term which is used in English to describe this inherited blemish—original sin—can be misleading, first of all because this sin is not original to the person (but comes from Adam) and secondly because it is not sin in the sense of an actual sin which is committed with personal consent. Rather this sin "infects" without consent and is also forgiven without consent in baptism. The Second Council of Orange in 529 called original sin "the death of the soul".

Although original sin is wiped out in baptism, its consequences remain, in an inherent weakness and inclination toward evil.

At the dawn of human history, then, the soul was utopian in the most accessible sense of that word. Adam and Eve were in possession of perfect and complete souls and were united to God by his grace. This was through no achievement of theirs; it was a pure gift which they enjoyed. After the Fall this utopia became inaccessible, symbolized by the cherubim and the fiery sword stationed to guard access to the tree of life (Genesis 3:24). The souls of the first couple became deformed and disfigured by sin, losing the splendour they once so easily possessed.

Through the sacrifice of Christ, the second Adam, who died on the cross, thus throwing open the way to God through this new tree of life, utopia once again opens for the soul, this time through the re-creation of redemption.

Adam's sinful disobedience barred the way to paradise; Christ's holy obedience unlocks the door. The new utopia inaugurated by Christ is characterized by an unambiguous realism: although baptism restores life to the soul, so that this new-found communion with God becomes its fortress, this sacrament does not wipe out the consequences of original sin and so the person remains a fragile soul. Because the human soul has been recreated by grace, it is beautiful and utopian once again; because this treasure is carried in an earthen vessel (2 Corinthians 4:7), each human being needs to realize that this power is God's and that this utopian condition is not a sure or certain possession because of his or her own weakness.

If creation of the soul was the first utopia, and the re-creation of the soul by virtue of Christ's redemption is the second utopia, then the third utopia is the perfection of the soul which can be seen in the lives of saints, who have brought re-creation to the highest level possible. The saints, both canonised and uncanonised, have achieved the utopia of perfection through God's grace and their good will. They have emptied themselves of the pride of egoism and the struggle for their own interests, and instead reach out in love to their neighbour. They attain a level of goodness that many people find difficult to imagine: giving up their lives out of love of God and for the sake of their sisters and brothers (John 15:13). This makes them like God, because it elevates them to the fullness of love.

But are the lives of the saints merely impeccable testimonies to a privatised charity? No, because a perfect soul is not an isolated entity but a social being with a social impact. Implicit within the lives of the saints is a programme for a different and better kind of society, one that is utopian in the purest sense of the word, because it is perfect. The saints are already living a future which is radically different from our present. Although this future may seem humanly impossible, they have made this "nowhere" into a "somewhere", thereby demonstrating that it is not in fact beyond the parameters of the possible because "nothing is impossible with God" (Luke 1:37). And they have entered this future without compromising their human nature, though they have transcended the strongly centripetal force that keeps the self revolving around its own interests and concerns. The saintly utopia is not socially imposed through laws, sanctions and punishments, but achieved through their free response to the love of God turned toward them and inviting them into communion. This generous response spills over into the rest of society. By living the Gospel Beatitudes (Matthew 5:3-12; Luke 6:20-26) and exigencies of the Sermon on the Mount within which the Beatitudes are incorporated (Matthew 5:1-7:29), these Christians challenge the surrounding social matrix to alter its priorities and re-configure its structure.

The Sermon on the Mount, which is at the core of Jesus' teaching, shows the way of the perfect soul. The perplexing promises and mind-boggling blessings that are the Beatitudes show how to achieve happiness and perfection. The entire Sermon on the Mount spells out the Christian utopia, since its implementation could radically reform society. But the Sermon on the Mount does not make sense without Christ. Without him, it is far-fetched and fantasy-like, preposterous and even absurd.

The Beatitudes demonstrate what a truly Christian life involves. Many people cannot envisage as hopeful the situations that Jesus describes as blessed in the Beatitudes. This is because of a failure of imagination, no doubt a result of the fact that original sin contaminates human reason, urging it to equate happiness with prosperity, great sex, gourmet food, celebrity status, and so on. Despite sustained empirical evidence, there is an inability to recognize that these factors, although bringing pleasure, do not bring joy that is deep enough to satisfy, or happiness that lasts. The human imagination finds it challenging to see that happiness might be in an unexpected place. Jesus, who came not to give partial life but full life (John 10:10), pointed out that the fullness of life is not where most people might like it to be. In the Beatitudes, he shows where this abundant life can be found by giving a concrete list of attitudes and actions, of dispositions and destinies that make people blessed.

Jesus blesses the spiritually poor person who has demolished the illusions of independence and self-sufficiency, and instead constantly looks to God for help. He blesses as well the person who lives simply from a socio-economic point of view—the poor are without doubt his favourites, the most forgotten are the ones he remembers most fondly. A rich person who lives for money destroys the greatest wealth, which is the soul. However, a poor person who hates rich people because of their possessions is also on a course of self-destruction. Poverty of spirit means not making wealth, success, fame, friendship, romance, marriage, learning, self, or career into gods. The commandment of God is to love only him with all of one's being, and to love others as oneself, but not as much as him. Jesus proclaims those who hunger for justice to be happy because living justly is what nourishes and strengthens the soul just as living healthily enhances the body. Jesus blesses those who weep and mourn, for this gives their hearts the mellowness of love and compassion that lets them reach out to their brothers and sisters. Jesus says the gentle are happy because they show kindness to others and do not judge them, but draw them toward goodness through their lowliness and love. The merciful are happy because they realise that everyone, most of all themselves, needs forgiveness. The pure in heart are blessed because their desire is only to see God in himself and to see him in all people and things. The peacemakers are happy because they radiate serenity and help to bring calm to troubled situations, averting the hatred that comes from conflict and war.

There are a couple of blessings among the Beatitudes that amount to a frank admission that the Gospel utopia, although conceivable, will not be realisable in global terms. This is not because this perfectly Christian society is essentially impossible. Although this type of social world is not out of the question, Jesus knows that people will not always use their freedom for the sake of goodness. These blessings relate to people who suffer because of their faith. Jesus promises joy for believers who are persecuted and calumniated. The good people who are persecuted are happy because the suffering of persecution enhances the beauty of their souls through their association with the blood of the Lamb. Those who are accused falsely because of their faith in God rejoice, because their faith gives them certainty that God judges truly and so they will be greatly rewarded in heaven.

As the Sermon on the Mount continues after the proclamation of the Beatitudes, Jesus gives simple commands about Christian life that are also thoroughly demanding to live out. He invites Christians to be the salt of the earth and the light of the world. To give the world a new flavour,

Christians need to constitute the crucial pinch of salt, by devoting themselves with undying loyalty and zest to the cause of the Gospel. To be light, Christians need to keep love aflame in their hearts. Christians are asked to present the other cheek to the one who strikes them, so that they can endure this violence in a spirit of love, rather than see the offender attack another person who would burn with anger and thirst for vengeance. If someone steals their mantle they are to offer their tunic also, so that the robber will not become a robber twice over. Christians are to practise absolute honesty, letting their yes be yes and their no be no: such integrity can transform society into a fabric of trust. Christian men are not to commit adultery in their hearts by looking at women with lust. Christians are not to "murder" others through venting their rage upon them. They are to love their enemies, to do good to those who hate them.

The clear-cut demands that Jesus imparts in the Sermon on the Mount would not be congenial either to the modern or the postmodern sensibility. The fortress soul of modernity would be loath to risk the vulnerable encounter that turning the other cheek, loving one's enemies, and a life of self-sacrificing service entails. Such commands would go against the rationality it prizes so highly, and would threaten to destroy an economic system built on competition, where personal greatness is measured by status and wealth. The fortress soul of modernity does not find it difficult to deny God. This is because it does not want to accept with humility what it cannot explain by reason alone. It falsely believes that such humble acceptance amounts to a belittlement of itself. The fragile or weak soul of the postmodern era has rejected large-scale truths and prefers a truth of its own making; it would rail against the simple yet absolute truth offered by Jesus in the Sermon on the Mount. It would delight in a lengthy flirtation with intriguing but tangential ideas in Jesus' teaching, before eventually opting for a mix and match Gospel, selecting those commands it could interpret in its own idiosyncratic and arbitrary manner. The fragile soul of postmodern sensibility finds it easy to accept God, as long as this God is a God of its own making and "un-making." Although Jacques Derrida, one of the leading postmodern thinkers, has turned toward religion, he regards it more as a passion for the impossible rather than a yearning for a God whose name can be spoken. In postmodern thinking there is a tendency to cover the simplicity of the divine (e.g. the truth that God is *agape*-love) with so many layers of superfluous verbiage, incidental etymological allusions, and convolutedly clever puns, that such thought ends up drawing attention most of all to its own stylistic inventiveness rather than actually engaging issues of real substance. But the loving soul understands that it is not enough to look at things with wisdom; one must also turn towards them with love. The one who loves will always find the truth.

It is not surprising that the blueprint Jesus offers in the Sermon on the Mount is not often enthusiastically embraced, since from a human point of view, this roadmap for life looks impossible. But at the same time, many people, both Christians and non-Christians, are inspired by this marvellous vision of a new humanity. Something within us, namely the human soul, intuitively knows that the Sermon on the Mount, for all its paradoxes and apparent absurdities, makes utter sense. The soul knows that these demands are viable because the soul refuses to accept the boundaries that society places on possibility. It yearns beyond what is actually given, it strives to step outside of (*ex-stasis*) the confines of its present self. In the Sermon on the Mount Jesus unveils a horizon of possibilities that is concealed in the actuality of the everyday. Quotidian life need not be endured in mediocrity and accepted with complacency; we can become the salt of the earth and the light of the world by piercing the present in order to disclose a better future. The utopian vision of Jesus does not stop at being a critique of society as we now know it; this vision does not rest content with encouraging us to go a reasonable distance further along the road of spiritual progress. More than offering simply a critical standard regarding the status quo and an invitation towards improvement, Jesus demands transformation. He asks Christians to realize, in a complete manner, perfect saintliness.

This total realization of the demands of Jesus begins with desire. The utopia of the Sermon on the Mount will never happen for people unless they want it to happen. Desires need to be re-discovered and renewed, re-educated and re-channelled. Christians need to desire in a deeper, fuller and newer way than they ever thought possible. As we saw in our discussion of *eros* in Plato's *Symposium*, love is a desire that is directed toward goodness and beauty, a desire that is perpetually restless and alive because it is never satisfied. Love always seeks more, and that is why it never comes to an end. Although aware of his human poverty because his mother is pure need, the character *Eros* also derives abundant energy from his father who is the god of resourcefulness. An analogous double nature is present in Christians who are dust of the earth yet "God-breathed," both earthen vessels and children of the Almighty.

The double nature of Christians is reflected in the twofold world they inhabit: the city of humanity and the city of God. Human society always falls short of the city of God. Because no culture has ever incarnated Christian utopia in a perfect way, many Christians over the centuries have set themselves apart from wider society in order to nourish the life of the soul through constructing their own religious utopias. St. Anthony and other early Christians fled to the desert in such numbers that these Desert Fathers made a city of the wilderness, and ever since monastic communities have been following their lead. In the early seventeenth century, Jesuits set up ideal societies of indigenous peoples in Latin America. These "reductions" in countries such as Paraguay and Brazil were an attempt "to reduce" or return to communal simplicity in economically autonomous and self-sufficient commonwealths; in the same century the Puritans who fled from religious persecution in Europe sought to create Christian utopias in places like Plymouth and New Haven. At their best these societies were caring rather than competitive, communal rather than individualistic, secure rather than unstable, reconciliatory rather than retributive.

But most Christians do not have the opportunity (or necessarily the desire) to set themselves apart from the world in a geographical and physical way. However, in order to journey with one's soul, there is at least the need to set oneself apart in a spiritual way. This does not mean retreating from the world into one's soul but becoming embedded in the world in a loving way with one's entire being, both soul and body. Jesus offers the example of someone fully living in the world while absolutely not colluding with its sinful dimension. Jesus offers utopia, a new way of being that cannot be achieved by one's unaided efforts, but which God can realize with the good will and co-operation of the human being.

This utopian model involves a whole human being, with an embodied soul and an animate body. In the figure of Jesus, body and soul, visible and invisible, outer and inner, are in harmony. Jesus constantly reveals unsuspected depths to those he meets in Palestine, yet this abyss of meaning always has a tangible and bodily expression. People touch Jesus because there is a power emanating from him. It is as though by touching his body they believe they will come into contact with his soul. Jesus reaches out his hand to heal the sick and he puts his hands on children to give them a spiritual blessing. Jesus asks the Samaritan woman at the well for some water to drink and offers her something to slake her spiritual thirst. The sign of the spiritual friendship between Jesus and the beloved disciple is revealed through the latter leaning against Jesus' breast during the Last Supper. This spiritual love that is expressed bodily is not only for the beloved disciple but especially for sinners. Jesus physically sits at table with tax collectors and sinners, and by virtue of eating and drinking alongside them Jesus invites them spiritually to satisfy the hunger and thirst of their souls for God. In the sixth chapter of John's Gospel Jesus offers his body and blood as food for the soul. His soul's sorrow reveals itself in his tears over Jerusalem and those he sheds at the death of his friend Lazarus. His spiritual agony in Gethsemane is revealed in the form of perspiration that falls from his body like drops of blood. His forgiving soul is sublimely expressed on the cross by the unforgettable words, "Father forgive them for they know not what they do." Even after the Resurrection, body and soul continue to work as a unity. Jesus appears bodily to the disciples, inviting Thomas to place his hand in his side so that this bodily contact will help his spirit to believe. Later the risen Jesus eats breakfast with a group of disciples on the shores of the Lake of Tiberias.

This small number of examples indicates the utter seriousness and nobility of the truth that the Word became flesh. The second person of the Trinity, the Word who was with God and who was God, became a human being. Jesus who was fully divine became fully human. He had a human soul and a human body. He assumed both soul and body, and redeemed both. None of the disciples saw the soul of Jesus, but they did see its bodily effects, in the way he spoke, listened, looked, touched, reasoned, acted, loved, suffered and prayed. Therefore Jesus was no spiritual abstraction. But neither was he a body empty of soul: the reason the evangelists report all the bodily deeds of Jesus is because they were "ensouled" actions, corporeal acts that were not lifeless and mechanical but full and vital. Because body and soul acted in unison, the body of Jesus is not an accidental or extraneous dimension of his being.

The Word became flesh for a specific reason: in order that human beings could share in the divine nature (2 Peter 1:4). Christ would like to permeate the being of each person so much that they can proclaim with Paul that "I no longer live, but Christ lives in me" (Galatians 2:20). It is not a matter of becoming God; only God is God. Each human being remains a creature. Nevertheless the perfect soul becomes perfectly conformed to the divine image and likeness. The soul's perfection depends neither on the length of its prayers nor the depth of its mystical insights nor the vastness of its theology. The source of its perfection is more concrete in nature: its treatment of the living bodies of others. According to the portrayal of the Last Judgement[100] in Matthew's Gospel (Matthew 25:31-46), the *only* practices of which God will demand an account on the last day are the following: feeding the hungry and giving drink to the thirsty, clothing the naked, taking in the stranger, visiting the sick, and visiting the imprisoned. This starkly simple vision of what it means to live the utopia of the soul is a straightforward recipe for greatness.

In Dostoevsky's *The Brothers Karamazov*, the holy monk Zosima recommends such committed love to a woman of little faith as a way to strengthen her belief in God and in the immortality of the soul:

> Strive to love your neighbour actively and indefatigably. Insofar as you advance in love you will grow surer of the reality of God and of the immortality of your soul. If you attain to perfect self-forgetfulness in the love of your neighbour, then you will believe without doubt, and no doubt can possibly enter your soul. This has been tried. This is certain.[101]

While the soul's path to perfection is unbelievably simple to understand (although demanding to put into practice), the soul itself will always be mysterious, like God from whom it originates. Should we just maintain a dignified and reserved silence about it as Wittgenstein suggested regarding those things about which we cannot speak? After all, it seems that by speaking of the soul we are simply betraying the depths of our ignorance. The great mysteries of life certainly cannot be communicated adequately by reason. Total comprehension of the soul is impossible.

Human understanding will ultimately fall short before the depth and breadth of this mystery. But the alternative to full understanding is not complete ignorance. In other words, there is a third way between the polarities of perfect knowledge and thoroughgoing unknowing. There is a kind of knowledge that is resistant to the precision and definition of conceptual elaboration. There is knowledge which is neither a grasping nor an encompassing of the object it seeks. There is knowledge which of its nature always remains incomplete. There is knowledge which is rarely conscious and seldom explicit. Or to put it more lyrically, "the heart has its reasons of which reason knows nothing" (Blaise Pascal). Pascal does not say that the heart is irrational; it has its reasons. We have all heard phrases such as "I know it in my heart" or "a gut feeling tells me," or in an even more colloquial manner people talk about "picking up the vibes". The heart "knows" more about the soul than reason can consciously articulate.

In this book I have tried to articulate some heart knowledge about the soul. We witnessed the intimacy of God's creation of the first human being in Genesis, how he took the dust of the earth and lovingly shaped it into a human form, before breathing the loving breath of life into its nostrils. We reflected on the startling gift of being made in God's image and likeness, and saw how this is a huge affirmation of the priceless nature of our soul and our body. We saw how death does not remove the soul from the world but makes it more present in an actively engaged immortality that is sustained by the divine dialogue of love initiated at creation, a dialogue that will have no end. We looked at how a good life beautifies the life of the soul and how the desire for beauty, rightly channelled, leads to God. If we are to find the beauty of God in our world, there turns out to be no surer one to behold than the crucified Jesus. Exploring paradigms of the soul in the contemporary world, we discovered the exclusive, isolated and suspicious fortress soul on the one hand, and the vulnerable and wounded soul on the other. If the self-centredness of the fortress soul is untenable from a Christian point of view, the fragile soul collapses under the weight of its own responsibility, tottering permanently on the edge of a nervous breakdown. I charted a way beyond the fortress and fragile soul through exploring the loving soul. The soul is created for the vast expanse of *agape*-love that originates in God, but because the whole person is both soul and body, *agape*-love will always live alongside *eros*-love. Finally we turned to the utopian soul. I suggested that Jesus lives this utopian model of the soul and offers us a concrete checklist so that we can transform this possibility from the distance of dreams to the closeness and concreteness of a lived reality.

I would like to end with a few words that express a deeply-felt personal conviction. The soul is the divine gem inside of us, a space of unfettered freedom that nobody can rob us of—except ourselves. Love is the life of the soul. If love grows cold, the soul dies to divine life. Because the soul is immaterial and invisible, this death can pass unnoticed. "The biggest danger, that of losing oneself, can pass off in the world as quietly as if it were nothing; every other loss, an arm, a leg, five dollars, a wife, etc., is bound to be noticed."[102] But the soul brims over with hope, precisely because there is something divine in it and that is why it cannot but yearn for God. Certainly this divine light dims to a glimmer when we become absorbed by solely material concerns. But it can be re-ignited more easily than we suppose.

If somebody loses an arm or a leg, it does not grow back. If someone loses a fortune, they must start again from scratch and put in enormous effort in order to regain anything. If somebody's wife dies he cannot turn the clock back and have her at his side again. But God's generosity defies human and temporal logic. Although the soul can die to love quietly and unnoticed, it can be reborn with astonishing speed. The parable of the workers in the vineyard (Matthew 20:1-16) teaches us that God pays those who arrive at the last minute the same reward as those who have laboured all day in the vineyard. My hope is that this book will be an encouragement to re-ignite this divine spark within, or to fan its flames if it is already glowing, and to warm it with love so that it will never be extinguished, but burn brightly and forever.

Notes

INTRODUCTION

1. The English translation is mine. The original Latin of Hadrian's poem is as follows:

> Animula vagula blandula
> Hospes comesque corporis
> Quae nunc abibis in loca
> Pallidula, rigida, nudula
> nec, ut soles, dabis iocos.

2. In a recent book, for instance, Thomas Moore writes, "A spirituality imbued with soul takes us profoundly into, through, and beyond this life." *The Soul's Religion: Cultivating a Profoundly Spiritual Way of Life*, London: Bantam Books, 2003, p. 306.

3. John O'Donohue, *Anam Cara: Spiritual Wisdom from the Celtic World*, London: Bantam Press, 1997.

4. Deepak Chopra, *How To Know God: The Soul's Journey Into the Mystery of Mysteries*, New York and London: Random House, 2001, p. 275.

5. Mary Midgley, for instance, argues with verve and panache that we humans are much more similar to animals than some of us might like to believe. See Mary Midgley, *Beast and Man: The Roots of Human Nature* (revised edition), London: Routledge, 1995.

6. Some people argue that animals are immortal. I must admit that I am not altogether at ease with the prospect of the billions of rats, cockroaches and mosquitoes that have populated our planet joining us in the afterlife! I contemplate this possibility with a mixture of trepidation and dismay, unless such animals undergo radical transformation (for instance, mosquitoes that no longer buzz and sting, but warble and caress). On the other hand, I can think of animals that I would be more than happy to greet in the next world, such as eagles, lambs and dolphins, to name only three.

7. Jean-Dominique Bauby, *The Diving Bell and the Butterfly: A Memoir of Life in Death*, translated by Jeremy Leggatt, New York: Alfred A. Knopf, 1997.

8. The fact that the animal is an inferior creature to the human being does not

mean that the animal is without value. Since animals are creatures of God, and thereby good, and are furthermore a gift from God to human beings to make their lives more enjoyable, the human being has a duty to be humane rather than inhuman towards the animal.

9. I am talking only about the earthly body here. The earthly body is suitable for life on earth; a similar yet radically different body is necessary in the after-life. The resurrected body will differ from the earthly body in that it will be imperishable, and not liable to the deterioration of age, declining health, and so on.

ONE: THE LIVING SOUL

10. The fact that God inspires biblical writers does not imply that God replaces them. Had God replaced them, the biblical books would be perfect works of art, which they manifestly are not. But God, although ensuring the truth of scripture, does not compel these writers to compose in a manner or style that is foreign to them.

11. Claus Westermann, "Leib und Seele in der Bibel", in *Was Weiss Man Von Der Seele? Erforschung und Erfahrung*, edited by Hans Jürgen Schultz, Stuttgart: Kreuz Verlag, 1967, p. 169.

12. Thomas Merton, *The Seven Storey Mountain* (Harcourt: San Diego and New York, 1999), p. 3. *The Seven Storey Mountain* was first published in 1948.

13. See Aristotle, *Nicomachean Ethics*, Book 8, Chapter 1.

TWO: IMAGE AND LIKENESS

14. Richard Kearney, *The Wake of Imagination: Toward a Postmodern Culture*, London: Routledge, 1994, pp. 5-6.

THREE: THE IMMORTAL SOUL

15. Apart from the principal issue of immortality versus resurrection, there are also question marks concerning Cullmann's stark dichotomy between Socrates and Jesus. For instance, we have mixed evidence concerning Socrates' belief in the immortality of the soul. In the early Platonic dialogue, the *Apology*, which is presumed to reflect with reasonable fidelity the views of Socrates himself, the latter shows himself to be unsure whether the soul will outlast death or not. It is true that Socrates provides proofs for the immortality of the soul in the *Phaedo*, but this middle-period dialogue is generally taken to express Plato's opinion rather than Socrates'. More importantly, Cullmann concludes from statements of Jesus such as "my soul is troubled, even to death," or synoptic descriptions of him as distressed and trembling, that the object of his distress and sorrow was death. However, it seems more plausible to me that Jesus' distress is due to other factors—the temptation that his death might be useless and of no value for humanity but above all the bitter and debilitating experience of shouldering both

humankind's "no" to God's love and God's "no" to humankind's rejection of his love.

16. Karl Barth, *The Doctrine of Creation (Church Dogmatics, Volume III, 2)*, translated by Harold Knight, G.W. Bromiley, J.K.S. Reid, R.H. Fuller, T. & T. Clark: Edinburgh, 1960, pp. 632-633.

17. See Thomas Nagel, "Death", in Thomas Nagel, *Mortal Questions*, Cambridge: Cambridge University Press, 1979, pp. 1-10.

18. Emmanuel Levinas, *Time and the Other [and additional essays]*, translated by Richard A. Cohen, Pittsburgh, Pa.: Duquesne University Press, 1987, p. 74.

19. Martin Heidegger, *Being and Time*, translated by John Macquarrie and Edward Robinson, Oxford: Basil Blackwell, 1962, p. 284.

20. Emmanuel Levinas, *Time and the Other*, p. 72.

21. Of course, the phenomenon of death also leads to humility in Heidegger's ontological analysis, since it reveals the authentic *Dasein*.

22. Emmanuel Levinas, *Time and the Other*, p. 74.

23. Plato, *Symposium*, 207d-e, translated by Alexander Nehamas and Paul Woodruff, in Plato, *Complete Works*, edited, with introduction and notes, by John M. Cooper, associate editor, D.S. Hutchinson, Indianapolis: Hackett Publishing Company, 1997, p. 490.

24. See for instance Saint Thomas of Aquinas, *Summa contra gentiles*, II, 57.

25. In fact Aquinas argued that the unity of the soul with matter was more intimate than the unity to be found between material things: "Quanto forma magis vincit materiam, ex ea et materia efficitur magis unum." *Ibid.*, II, 68.

26. For instance, discussing angels in relation to place in the *Summa Theologica*, Aquinas comments that an angel is in a place in a different sense from a body. An angel cannot be contained by a place since an incorporeal substance practically contains the thing which it comes in contact with. In a similar way the soul is in the body as containing the body rather than as being contained by it. See *Summa Theologica*, I, 52, 1.

27. This is because the human being is not only a soul, but is composed of body and soul. See *Ibid.*, I, 75, 4.

28. Aquinas provided numerous arguments for the survival of the soul after death. Towards the end of this chapter I will turn to Aquinas' argument for immortality that is based on the human desire to live forever.

29. For Aquinas' discussion of what the intellect knows in material things, see *Summa Theologica.*, I, 86.

30. This is well expressed by the scholastic adage: *nihil est in intellectu, quod prius non fuerit in sensu* ("nothing is in the intellect that was not first in the senses").

31. Karl Rahner, *Foundations of Christian Faith: An Introduction to the Idea of Christianity*, translated by William V. Dych, London: Darton, Longman & Todd, 1978, p. 30.

32. Although Rahner had enormous respect for Heidegger as a teacher, the latter did not constitute the most important philosophical influence upon Rahner's intellectual career. In a piece written for a *Festschrift* on Heidegger in 1969, Rahner, as one might expect in a book written as a tribute, described Heidegger's effect upon him in glowing terms: "I might very simply and modestly acknowledge that although I had many good professors in the classroom, there is only *one* whom I can revere as my teacher, and he is Martin Heidegger." (Reprinted in the preface to Thomas Sheehan's *Karl Rahner: The Philosophical Foundations*, Athens, Georgia: Open University Press, 1987, p. xi). However, in an interview with Leo O'Donovan ten years later in 1979, Rahner was more circumspect about Heidegger's influence: "Certainly I learned a variety of things from him [Heidegger], even if I have to say that I owe my most basic, decisive, philosophical direction, insofar as it comes from someone else, more, in fact, to the Belgian philosopher and Jesuit, Joseph Maréchal. His philosophy already moved beyond the traditional neoscholasticism. I brought that direction from Maréchal to my studies with Heidegger and it was not superseded by him." (Karl Rahner, *Karl Rahner in Dialogue: Conversations and Interviews*, 1965-1982, New York: Crossroad, 1986, p. 90).

33. *Spirit in the World* was first published in German as *Geist in Welt. Zur Metaphysik der endlichen Erkenntnis bei Thomas von Aquin*, Innsbruck: Rauch, 1939.

34. "Man faces his own death, and he knows this. As distinguished from the demise of an animal, this knowledge is itself a piece of his dying and of his death because it constitutes the precise difference between the death of a man and the demise of an animal, because only man exists always and inescapably confronted with his end, with the totality of his existence, with its temporal end." Karl Rahner, *Foundations of Christian Faith: An Introduction to the Idea of Christianity*, translated by William V. Dych, London: Darton, Longman & Todd, 1978, pp. 269-270.

35. See Karl Rahner, *Zur Theologie des Todes mit einem Exkurs über das Martyrium*, Freiburg: Verlag Herder, 1958, p. 22.

36. See Karl Rahner, *Zur Theologie des Todes*, p. 20.

37. Joseph Ratzinger, *Introduction to Christianity*, translated by J.R. Foster, San Francisco: Ignatius Press, 1990, p. 275.

38. *Ibid.*, p. 271.

39. ". . . only *one* could truly give lasting stability: he who *is,* who does not come into existence and pass away again but abides in the midst of transience: the God of the living, who does not just hold the shadow and echo of my being, whose ideas are not just copies of reality. I myself am his thought, which establishes me more securely, so to speak, then I am in myself; his thought is not the posthumous shadow but the original source and strength of my being." *Ibid.*, p. 232.

40. *Ibid.*, p. 271.

41. *Ibid.*, p. 234.
42. *Ibid.*, p. 274.

FOUR: BEAUTY AND THE SOUL

43. Saint Augustine, *Confessions*, translated with an introduction by Henry Chadwick, Oxford: Oxford University Press, 1991; Book X, viii, 15, p. 187.
44. *Ibid.*, Book X, xxvii, 38, p. 201.
45. This marvellous passage is worth quoting in full. "Turn now from man's mind to his body. It is true that it is no better than the body of a beast as far as dying is concerned and, in life, it is even weaker than that of many animals. Nevertheless, the human body is a revelation of the goodness of God and of the providence of the body's Creator. It is a body obviously meant to minister to a rational soul, as you can see from the arrangement of the human organs of sense and of man's other members. This is obvious, too, in man's specific appearance, form, and stature. The bodies of irrational animals are bent toward the ground, whereas man was made to walk erect with his eyes on heaven, as though to remind him to keep his thought on things above. And if we need further evidence to show to what kind of a mind the body was meant to minister, we have only to think of the marvellous mobility of the tongue and the hands, so perfectly suited for speaking and writing, for the arts, and for the countless other activities of men.

"What is more, quite apart from these practical purposes, there is in a man's body such a rhythm, poise, symmetry, and beauty that it is hard to decide whether it was the uses or the beauty of the body that the Creator had most in mind. It is clear that every organ whose function we know adds to the body's beauty, and this beauty would be still more obvious if only we knew the precise proportions by which the parts were fashioned and interrelated. I do not mean merely the surface parts which, no doubt, could be accurately measured by anyone with proper skill. I mean the parts hidden below our skin, the intricate complex of veins and nerves, the inmost elements of the human viscera and vital parts, whose rhythmic relationships have not yet been revealed. Surgeons, of course, have done something in their relatively crude anatomical study of corpses (and in the course of their hardly less inhuman operations on living bodies) to explore the last recesses of the organs they have had to handle in order to learn the best technique in dealing with this or that disorder. But what I have in mind is the rhythm of relationships, the *harmonia*, as the Greeks would say, whereby the whole body, inside and out, can be looked upon as a kind of organ with a music all its own. The beauty of this music no one has yet discovered, because no one has dared look for it. Nevertheless, if this total organic design could only be discerned, even in the seemingly ugly elements of the human viscera, there would be revealed to the soul so ravishing a beauty that no visible shapeliness of form that delights the eye—the mere minister of the mind—could be compared with it.

"Of course, some parts of the human body appear to have no other purpose than to add to beauty, as the mamillae on a man's chest or the beard on his face. Certainly, if the beard was meant for protection rather than for beauty, it would have served a better purpose for the weaker sex, whose face remains uncovered. If, then, we argue from the facts, first, that, as everyone admits, not a single visible organ of the body serving a definite function is lacking in beauty, and, second, that there are some parts which have beauty and no apparent function, it follows, I think, that in the creation of the human body God put form before function. After all, function will pass and the time will come when we shall delight solely in the unlibidinous contemplation of one another's beauty, knowing that our joy will be giving glory to the Creator, of whom the Psalmist says: 'Thou hast put on praise and beauty.'" Saint Augustine, *The City of God, Books XVII-XXII,* translated by Gerald G. Walsh and Daniel J. Honan, Washington, D.C.: The Catholic University of America Press, 1981; Book XXII, Chapter 24, pp. 485-487.

46. Saint Augustine, *The City of God, Books I-VII,* translated by Demetrius B. Zema and Gerald G. Walsh, with an introduction by Etienne Gilson, Washington, D.C.: The Catholic University of America Press in association with Consortium Books, 1977; Book I, Chapter 13, p. 40.

47. It is in his treatise on the Trinity that Augustine describes the image of God within us as comprising memory, understanding and will. See for instance: "By making use also of the creature which God has made, insofar as we could, we have warned those, who demand the reason concerning such things, that they should behold the invisible things of Him through those that were made, especially through that rational or intellectual creature which was made to the image of God; through which, as through a mirror, they would behold, insofar as they would be able, if indeed they would be able, that God who is Trinity in our memory, understanding, and will." Saint Augustine, *The Trinity,* translated by Stephen McKenna, Washington: The Catholic University of America Press, 1963; Book XV, Chapter 20, 39, pp. 505-506.

48. Saint Augustine, *Confessions,* Book X, xvii, 26, p. 194.

49. James Joyce, *A Portrait of the Artist as a Young Man,* edited with an introduction and notes by Seamus Deane, London: Penguin Books, 2000, p. 3.

50. "There exists another power, not only that by which I give life to my body but also that by which I enable its senses to perceive . . . I who act through these diverse functions am one mind." Saint Augustine, *Confessions,* Book X, vii, 11, p. 185.

51. "I asked myself why I approved of the beauty of bodies, whether celestial or terrestrial, and what justification I had for giving an unqualified judgement on mutable things, saying 'This ought to be thus, and that ought not to be thus'. In the course of this inquiry when I made such value judgements as I was making, I found the unchangeable and authentic eternity of truth to transcend my mutable mind." *Ibid.,* Book VII, xvii, 23, p. 127.

A similar kind of spiritual knowledge that is independent of the senses is also found in Joyce's character Stephen Dedalus, though Joyce's words leave us wondering whether we are really dealing with a form of superior knowledge or simply the blindness of a self-absorbed mind: "His thinking was a dusk of doubt and selfmistrust lit up at moments by the lightnings of intuition, but lightnings of so clear a splendour that in those moments the world perished about his feet as if it had been fireconsumed: and thereafter his tongue grew heavy and he met the eyes of others with unanswering eyes for he felt that the spirit of beauty had folded around him like a mantle and that in revery at least he had been acquainted with nobility." James Joyce, *A Portrait of the Artist as a Young Man*, p. 191.

52. Saint Augustine, *Confessions*, Book IX, x, 25, p. 172. What is especially striking about this illumination is that it is not an individual experience but a communal one, shared by both Monica and Augustine. Furthermore it reaches beyond time, since it is the next life and not the present one about which they are conversing. The vision bears good fruits, convincing Augustine that the pleasures of the world are as nothing compared to the eternal joy of being with God. It bestows a lasting peace upon him and imbues him with hope.

53. "But I was an unhappy young man, wretched as at the beginning of my adolescence when I prayed you for chastity and said: 'Grant me chastity and continence, but not yet.' I was afraid you might hear my prayer quickly, and that you might too rapidly heal me of the disease of lust which I preferred to satisfy rather than suppress." *Ibid.*, Book VIII, vii, 17, p. 145.

54. James Joyce, *A Portrait of the Artist as a Young Man*, p. 186.

55. *Ibid.*, p. 260.

56. Saint Augustine, *Confessions*, Book X, vi, 8, p. 183.

57. "In other words, syllogisms may still dutifully clatter away like rotary presses or computers which infallibly spew out an exact number of answers by the minute. But the logic of these answers is itself a mechanism which no longer captivates anyone. The very conclusions are no longer conclusive. And if that is how the transcendentals fare because one of them has been banished, what will happen with Being itself?" Hans Urs von Balthasar, *The Glory of the Lord: A Theological Aesthetics. Volume 1: Seeing the Form,* translated by Erasmo Leiva-Merikakis, Edinburgh: T. & T. Clark, 1982, p. 19.

58. Sophocles, *The Three Thebean Plays: Antigone, Oedipus the King, Oedipus at Colonus*, translated by Robert Fagles, introduction and notes by Bernard Knox, London and New York: Penguin Classics, 1984, lines 649 to 650, p. 319.

59. Sophocles, *Ajax*, translation and commentary by Shomit Dutta, introduction to Greek Theatre by P.E. Easterling, Cambridge: Cambridge University Press, 2001, p. 99.

60. Quoted in Sophocles, *Philoctetes*, translation and commentary by Judith Affleck, introduction to Greek Theatre by P.E. Easterling, Cambridge: Cambridge University Press, 2001, p. 104.

FIVE: BEYOND THE FORTRESS SOUL AND THE FRAGILE SOUL

61. See Paul Ricoeur, *Oneself as Another*, translated by Kathleen Blamey, Chicago and London: The University of Chicago Press, 1992, pp. 4-16.

62. According to Freud, it is not easy to admit "that the ego is not master in its own house" [*dass das Ich nicht Herr sei in seinem eigenen Haus*] since it is a "blow to man's self-love." Sigmund Freud, "A Difficulty in the Path of Psychoanalysis," *The Standard Edition of the Complete Psychological Works of Sigmund Freud*, Volume XVII, 1917-1919, translated by James Strachey in collaboration with Anna Freud, assisted by Alix Strachey and Alan Tyson, London: The Hogarth Press and the Institute of Psychoanalysis, 1955, p. 143.

63. *Roland Barthes by Roland Barthes*, translated by Richard Howard, London: The Macmillan Press Ltd., 1977, p. 56.

64. "on peut bien parier que l'homme s'effacerait, comme à la limite de la mer un visage de sable." Michel Foucault, *Les Mots et les choses*, Paris: NRF-Gallimard, 1966, p. 398.

65. Ciaran Benson, *The Cultural Psychology of Self: Place, Morality and Art in Human Worlds*, London: Routledge, 2001.

66. Richard Kearney, *Dialogues with Contemporary Thinkers*, Manchester: Manchester University Press, 1984, p. 125.

67. Emmanuel Levinas, *Otherwise than Being or Beyond Essence*, translated by Alphonso Lingis, Dordrecht, Boston, London: Kluwer Academic Publishers, 1991, p. xliii.

68. Emmanuel Levinas, "God and Philosophy," *Of God Who Comes to Mind*, translated by Bettina Burgo, Stanford: Stanford University Press, p. 72.

69. "In divesting the ego of its imperialism, the hetero-affection establishes a new undeclinability: the self, subjected to an absolute accusative, as though this accusation which it does not even have to assume came from it. The self involved in the *gnawing away at oneself* in responsibility, which is also incarnation, is not an objectification of the self by the ego." Emmanuel Levinas, Otherwise than Being or Beyond Essence *Otherwise than Being or Beyond Essence*, p. 121.

70. *Ibid.*, p. 110.

71. Emmanuel Levinas, *Totality and Infinity: An Essay on Exteriority*, translated by Alphonso Lingis, Pittsburgh: Duquesne University Press, pp. 199-200.

72. Joseph Ratzinger, *Introduction to Christianity*, p. 274.

73. Emmanuel Levinas, *Otherwise than Being or Beyond Essence*, p. 25.

74. *Ibid.*, p. 111.

75. *Ibid.*, p. 49.

76. *Ibid.*

77. *Ibid.*, p. 106.

78. Levinas is almost certainly aware of the Latin etymology of the word "obsession": *obsessus*—besieged.
79. Emmanuel Levinas, *Otherwise than Being or Beyond Essence*, p. 84.
80. *Ibid.*, p. 48.
81. *Ibid.*, p. 58.
82. *Ibid.*, p. 59.
83. *Ibid.*
84. *Ibid.*, p. 50.
85. From the poem "Do Not Go Gentle into That Good Night" by Dylan Thomas.
86. Emmanuel Levinas, *Otherwise than Being or Beyond Essence*, p. 108.
87. *Ibid.*, p. 75.
88. *Ibid.*, p. 79.
89. *Ibid.*, p. 116.

SIX: THE LOVING SOUL

90. Bernard Lonergan, *Method in Theology*, New York: Herder and Herder, 1972, p. 240.
91. Jürgen Moltmann, *The Crucified God: The Cross of Christ as the Foundation and Criticism of Christian Theology*, translated by R.A. Wilson and John Bowden, New York: Harper & Row, 1974, p. 7.
92. "As the whole of nature is akin, and the soul has learned everything, nothing prevents a man, after recalling one thing only—a process men call learning—discovering everything else for himself, if he is brave and does not tire of the search, for searching and learning are, as a whole, recollection." Plato, *Meno*, 81d, translated by G.M.A. Grube, in Plato, *Complete Works*, edited, with introduction and notes, by John M. Cooper, associate editor, D.S. Hutchinson, Indianapolis: Hackett Publishing Company, 1997, p. 880.
93. The fact that Diotima is a priestess is indicated both by her mediating role in averting a plague by instructing Athenians what sacrifices to make (*Symposium* 201d) and the fact that she talks to Socrates about initiating him into the rites of love (*Symposium* 210a).
94. Plato, *Symposium*, 202e, translated by Alexander Nehamas and Paul Woodruff, in Plato, *Complete Works*, edited, with introduction and notes, by John M. Cooper, associate editor, D.S. Hutchinson, Indianapolis: Hackett Publishing Company, 1997, p. 486.
95. *Ibid.*, 203c, p. 486.
96. *Ibid.*, 203c-d, p. 486.
97. *Ibid.*, 203d, p. 486.
98. *Ibid.*, 203e, p. 486.
99. *Ibid.*, 212a, p. 494.

SEVEN: THE UTOPIAN SOUL

100. The general, though not unanimous, consensus among scripture scholars is that the Last Judgement represents the authentic teaching of Jesus. According to Manson, the astounding originality of the Last Judgement already provides strong evidence that it goes back to Jesus himself. T.W. Manson, *The Sayings of Jesus as Recorded in the Gospels According to St. Matthew and St. Luke*, London: SCM Press, 1961, p. 249.

101. Fyodor Dostoevsky, *The Brothers Karamazov*, translated by Constance Garnett and revised by Ralph E. Matlaw, New York and London: W.W. Norton and Company, 1976, p. 48.

102. Søren Kierkegaard, *The Sickness Unto Death*, translated with an introduction by Alastair Hannay, London: Penguin Books, 1989, pp. 62-63.

Bibliography

Aquinas, Thomas, *The Summa Theologica*, translated by the Fathers of the English Dominican Province, 5 volumes, Westminster: Maryland: Christian Classics, 1981.

Augustine, *Confessions*, translated with an introduction by Henry Chadwick, Oxford: Oxford University Press, 1991.

Augustine, *The City of God, Books I-VII*, translated by Demetrius B. Zema and Gerald G. Walsh, with an introduction by Etienne Gilson, Washington, D.C.: The Catholic University of America Press in association with Consortium Books, 1977.

Augustine, *The City of God, Books XVII-XXII*, translated by Gerald G. Walsh and Daniel J. Honan, Washington, D.C.: The Catholic University of America Press, 1981.

von Balthasar, Hans Urs, *The Glory of the Lord: A Theological Aesthetics. Volume 1: Seeing the Form*, translated by Erasmo Leiva-Merikakis, Edinburgh: T. & T. Clark, 1982.

Barth, Karl, *The Doctrine of Creation* (Church Dogmatics, Volume III, 2), translated by Harold Knight, G.W. Bromiley, J.K.S. Reid, R.H. Fuller, T. & T. Clark: Edinburgh, 1960.

Bauby, Jean-Dominique, *The Diving Bell and the Butterfly: A Memoir of Life in Death*, translated by Jeremy Leggatt, New York: Alfred A. Knopf, 1997.

Joyce, James, *A Portrait of the Artist as a Young Man*, edited with an introduction and notes by Seamus Deane, London: Penguin Books, 2000,

Levinas, Emmanuel, *Time and the Other* [and additional essays], translated by Richard A. Cohen, Pittsburgh, Pa.: Duquesne University Press, 1987.

——*Otherwise than Being or Beyond Essence*, translated by Alphonso Lingis, Dordrecht, Boston, London: Kluwer Academic

Publishers, 199.

Lonergan, Bernard, *Method in Theology*, New York: Herder and Herder, 1972.

Merton, Thomas, *The Seven Storey Mountain*, Harcourt: San Diego and New York, 1999.

Plato, *Symposium, 207d-e*, translated by Alexander Nehamas and Paul Woodruff, in Plato, Complete Works, edited, with introduction and notes, by John M. Cooper, associate editor, D.S. Hutchinson, Indianapolis: Hackett Publishing Company, 1997, pp. 457-505.

Rahner, Karl, *Foundations of Christian Faith: An Introduction to the Idea of Christianity*, translated by William V. Dych, London: Darton, Longman & Todd, 1978.

———*Zur Theologie des Todes mit einem Exkurs über das Martyrium*, Freiburg: Verlag Herder, 1958.

Ratzinger, Joseph, *Introduction to Christianity*, translated by J.R. Foster, San Francisco: Ignatius Press, 1990.

Ricoeur, Paul, *Oneself as Another*, translated by Kathleen Blamey, Chicago and London: The University of Chicago Press, 1992.

Index